CHORAL CONDUCTING
An
Anthology

CHORAL CONDUCTING
An
Anthology

SECOND EDITION

SAMUEL ADLER
Eastman School of Music
The University of Rochester

SCHIRMER BOOKS
A Division of Macmillan, Inc.
NEW YORK

Collier Macmillan Publishers
LONDON

Schirmer Books
A Division of Macmillan, Inc.
866 Third Avenue, New York, N. Y. 10022

Collier Macmillan Canada, Inc.

Library of Congress Catalog Card Number: 84-759665

Printed in the United States of America

printing number
1   2   3   4   5   6   7   8   9   10

Library of Congress Cataloging in Publication Data
Main entry under title:
Choral conducting.

   1. Conducting, Choral.   2. Choruses.   I. Adler,
Samuel
MT85.C44   1985   84-759665
ISBN 0-02-870070-8

Contents

APPENDIXES

List of Compositions

CHAPTER 1

The One Beat

The Two Beat

The Three Beat

The Four Beat

CHAPTER 3

CHAPTER 4

CHAPTER 5

CHAPTER 6

CHAPTER 7

CHAPTER 8

Preface
to Second Edition

When a book has been in print for slightly over a dozen years, many comments and suggestions filter back to the author. I consider it a privilege and a rare opportunity to be able to publish a new and expanded edition in which it is possible to incorporate many of the extremely helpful critiques about the book and its usage sent to me by many good colleagues. The enthusiastic response to the anthology has been most heartening and I hope that the additions and revisions in this edition will go a long way toward fulfilling its mission of serving our college choral community even more effectively.

This volume now contains many more examples, especially in the early and more basic chapters. Further, I have heeded the criticism of many and have included shorter excerpts, since class time is always limited and it is extremely important that as many class members as possible get frequent exposure to the actual conducting of the group. For similar reasons, I have eliminated most works that cannot possibly be performed in a class situation because the required forces are too large or the work is so difficult to perform that an inordinate amount of time would have to be spent on problems having little value to all except the most advanced and experienced conductor. This is especially true of the examples that were in chapters 7 and 8. While I feel that every choral conductor should study and try to master the techniques of presenting the works of composers such as Lutoslawski, Penderecki, Ligeti, Nono, and Roger Reynolds, too much time is required for their preparation, and unfortunately that amount of time is unavailable in our choral conducting classes. Therefore, shorter and less complex excerpts were substituted for some of these brilliant works. Yet the newly incorporated works do present the student with similar problems and will prepare him or her to undertake performances of the more extensive pieces later on.

I would hope that the same strategies that have proven so successful with this book in the past would continue to be used. Thus far the most successful method has been that of each student having an anthology and different excerpts being assigned for conducting, rehearsing, and perfecting in a given time slot. I would like to recommend one fine suggestion which has been sent to me by many colleagues using this volume: it can be used as a guide to choral literature. I fully concur with this method and would urge the instructor to accept this added usage in order to give more depth to the study of choral conducting. When an excerpt is assigned to a student, he or she should be asked to research the life and style of its composer and perhaps to look into the other music of that particular person and masters who were his colleagues and possibly influences. In this manner, a great breadth of knowledge can be obtained and the student's repertoire will be greatly expanded. It may also be helpful for those bibliographies and short stylistic statements written by the students to be duplicated so that each member of the class could keep a notebook containing pertinent information about all the excerpts covered, even though many of them have not been assigned to the particular students as a conducting exercise.

Many thanks to Schirmer Books and especially to Maribeth Anderson Payne, senior editor, and Michael Sander, associate editor, for giving me the opportunity to republish the anthology. In conclusion, I wish to express my gratitude to the many loyal colleagues who have used the book and who have given me so much invaluable advice toward its revision.

Samuel Adler
Rochester, New York 1985

Preface
to First Edition

Choral Conducting: An Anthology is not intended to be a textbook in the ordinary sense of the word, for it is my conviction that even though there are several excellent books about conducting on the market today, none provides a body of musical material for the practical realization of the principles set forth. This is especially true of the books dealing with choral conducting. For this reason, I have endeavored to keep my comments on technique as well as those concerning each work to a minimum. These comments are structured as hints and general bits of information to aid the student and the instructor in the use of this volume.

The main purposes of this anthology are two: First, to provide a large body of choral music for use in conducting classes, since inadequate library facilities, unable to provide an instructor with multiple copies of desired works for use, often restrict the scope and the quality of the music available to realize the best results in these courses. The second major purpose is to suggest a structured curriculum which, if diligently pursued, will result in a practical and meaningful program for the acquisition of solid technique in the field of choral conducting.

The limited material available does not provide the student with a variety of music from all creative periods; further, this material denies him a conducting experience with many works of the past and, more specifically, with works of the twentieth century. The conducting problems seldom encountered in older music are only mentioned in class and seldom if ever actually conducted because of the unavailability of scores. I have tried to choose a variety of works from the great choral literature dating back to pre-Renaissance and including the late 1960s with the hope that exposure to individual pieces of many styles, periods, and composers will whet the student's as well as the instructor's appetite and prompt both to investigate all idioms in depth. This volume need not be the only material used in the classroom, but it certainly will provide a fertile base for a broadening of taste as well as conducting technique.

During the past two decades, we have witnessed a tremendous growth in choral activities especially in this country, and the choral literature is being nurtured constantly by significant works which not only demand a choral conductor possessing the gift of superior musicianship and interpretive powers, but also one having a faultless "stick" technique. (The word "stick" is in quotes for I use this term figuratively to mean the right-hand technique. I do not advocate the necessity of conducting a chorus with a baton. This option should be the instructor's. I think a student should be trained to be able to conduct both with and without a stick.)

It is because of the need for flawless technique that the three first and longest chapters have been devoted to "beat" problems. Exercises utilizing all the common beat patterns are plentifully represented and ordered in a graduated fashion, so that the examples in $\frac{4}{4}$ time range from relatively simple music to sounds of great complexity. Similar means are employed for each of the rhythmic patterns. The exercises will stress music with a variety of expressive feelings also, so that the nature of the beat may translate the dynamics and expression marks within the particular pattern. In order to further orient the student, diagrams of the commonly accepted beat patterns are provided as a reminder and guide.

Most works quoted are incomplete, for I felt that, rather than concentrate on one piece, it would be more interesting and educationally more stimulating for the student to practice the same patterns on diverse examples of compositional techniques. Each particular work is photographed in the edition in which it is available so that the student may become accustomed to the many different styles of printing on the market today. In this connection, I certainly do invite research on the part of the student into other editions of older works quoted in the anthology and critical discussion of the strengths and weaknesses of the various versions. In order to make the anthology uniform in size, some works were reduced and others enlarged. The printing was not changed.

Two more considerations should be mentioned. Generally, the music chosen is for four-part mixed chorus. This is for pragmatic purposes because choral conducting classes are not overly large and a four-voice texture would probably result in the best sound, since all parts may be adequately represented.

Because of the wealth of the original choral repertoire, I have purposely refrained from using arrangements except where unique examples of choral problems were manifested. The collector of an anthology always runs a great risk of offending taste or of being accused by many different schools of thought of omitting important examples illustrating one point or another. I cannot begin to defend myself on this score except to express the hope that the instructor will be able to lead the student to many more examples of the types quoted in this book. The selections included in this volume were chosen for the conducting problems inherent within them rather than for stylistic reasons.

The ideal use of this anthology is in a choral conducting class in which the four voice parts, soprano, contralto, tenor and bass, are represented. Each student should have a copy of the anthology and perform while his fellow classmates are conducting. The patterns should be diligently practiced in and out of class, with and without a baton. When they are mastered each student should have an opportunity to conduct at least one example in each portion of every chapter of the book.

Every student should analyze each example, both from a musical and a choral viewpoint. By the latter, I mean an analysis of possible difficulties that may arise in the performance of the works, either rhythmically, aurally, vocally or by any combination of these. In extreme situations the student should be encouraged to create exercises structured to overcome difficult conditions. A series of such exercises has been prepared for three excerpts that present a chorally problematic situation. These examples should be studied carefully, not necessarily imitated. The choral conductor must know his capabilities and problems as well as those of his group and thus create helpful passages which will aid his singers to overcome all musical trials.

Musical analysis of a particular piece should include stylistic, melodic, contrapuntal, harmonic, as well as timbral and even biographical or historical facts. The more knowledgeable a student is about the musical content of a work, the easier it will be for him to communicate its interpretation to a chorus.

Because of the disparity of ideas on conducting and interpretative practices, I have limited my written comments to introductory remarks at the beginning of each chapter. These will include information about the works and their composers and pose problems or give hints to be pondered, then solved in performance. This gives a great deal of freedom to the instructor and to the student. However, as mentioned previously, I hope that each example will contain enough problems and evoke discussion to such a point that all will want to study further the entire work and even take a closer look at the music of that particular composer, as well as more music in that idiom.

One practical note about the form of some of the examples. At times, I have chosen to begin an excerpt in the middle of a line to give a picture of what has immediately preceded it; consequently some previous measures were retained in the printing. In these cases, an arrow has been inserted to indicate where the actual conducting of the exercise should begin.

The compiling of this anthology was made easier by the gracious help and encouragement of several people. For the typing and correcting of this manuscript, I am indebted to my secretary Margaret Long. I consider the help received in the preparation and editing of the book invaluable, and want to express my gratitude especially to Ruth Chapman and Buryl Red of Holt, Rinehart and Winston for their marvelous work and support. This volume could not have been written without the kind cooperation of the many publishers who were willing to grant permission for the use of excerpts from their publications; a list of their names appears at the end of the book.

S. A.

Rochester, New York
June 1971

APPROACHES
to
RIGHT-HAND
TECHNIQUES

1
Simple and Compound Meters

Conducting is an act of communication, and as such utilizes certain tools to make itself understood. As words communicate, so do certain basic types of conducting gestures. They form a vocabulary which results in the clear transmission of musical ideas from the conductor to his chorus or orchestra.

The first purpose of conducting then is to present the metric course of the music to a group. While the basic conductorial beat patterns are more or less traditional, one should not use these to the extreme of becoming a human metronome. However, the first steps to perfect freedom of gestures are through strict adherence to traditional gestures until they become second nature and take on the personality of the conductor. It is for this reason that most of this anthology, and this first chapter in particular, concentrates on right-hand technique in order to nurture a beat which in the end is free of ambiguities and vital in its transmission of the rhythm, dynamics, and general expressive feeling of the music.

To strengthen the technique of the right hand the student should disregard the functions of the left hand in the exercises of the first three chapters. Some of these functions are to aid the right in climaxes, in tempo changes, as well as in the giving of cues and the signalling of dynamic changes. Later chapters will discuss the left hand more fully. Some examples given in the first three chapters will be repeated in Chapter 4 with special emphasis on the role of the left hand.

After each beat pattern has been thoroughly mastered with and without a baton, the following items must be given the most careful consideration and applied to each beat pattern before the exercises are conducted.

The Conductor's Beat Patterns

Diagrams cannot adequately represent the conductor's motions (gestures), especially the multitude of loops and expressive sweeps which become his very personal embellishments of the basic beat patterns as a conductor matures. Furthermore, musical situations and considerations of each work performed certainly govern the size and shape of the beat, but the traditional directions of each pattern should be utilized to ensure a uniform means of communication.

There is another musical consideration which should influence the decision of the conductor as to the size, shape, and nature of his beat and his beat pattern. This factor is tempo. The "tempo mark" is a relatively new innovation.

During the thirteenth and the fourteenth centuries the unit of time called *tempus* and the proportional notation resulting from this "normal beat" established an accepted tempo. We know that in the course of these centuries the note value of the basic *tempus* shifted from the *longa* to the *brevis* to the *semibrevis* and so on. The *tactus* of the fifteenth and the sixteenth centuries was the term used for the "conductor's beat," but there was a difference between our concept of beat and the meaning of the term *tactus*. Tactus was a relatively fixed duration of time equivalent to the metronome marking 50–60. All tempi were determined from the "normal tempo" or the tactus, from which only slight deviations were possible. Faster or slower tempi were brought about by proportioning the notation. A great deal has been written and much speculative controversy has been engendered by the tempo markings of the seventeenth and eighteenth centuries before the invention of the metronome.[1] It may be noted that during these centuries presto did not signify the "extremely quick" speed with which we perform our modern presto movements, and that this extreme speed did not come into vogue until the time of Mozart. When one encounters an unedited work with no modern metronome markings, inscribed simply with an Italian tempo mark, a good criterion should be the consideration of realizing the music with clarity so that neither the melodic movement nor the counterpoint are in any way obscured or distorted.

Today of course practically all works bear both a tempo marking as well as an equivalent metronome mark. These factors determine the tempo and combined with the character and dynamics of a particular work must finally decide the size and general condition of the conductor's gesture. Depending on the tempo or metronome marking $\frac{3}{2}, \frac{3}{4}, \frac{3}{8}, \frac{3}{16}$ may demand the same length of a beat. Similar decisions must be concluded as to the subdivision of a beat in an exceedingly slow tempo or the combining of several beats in one stroke at a fast pace ($\frac{3}{4}$ in 1 or $\frac{5}{4}$ in 2, and so on).

---

[1] For a thorough discussion of this subject it is strongly urged that the student refer to the book *Rhythm and Tempo* by Curt Sachs, New York: W. W. Norton Company, Inc., 1953.

Here without any more comment are the most commonly used conductor's gestures to be used when the musical situations warrant their application:

1. Directon of the beat patterns:

a. The Two beat: Two divided

   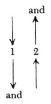

b. The Three beat   Three divided

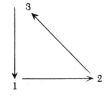   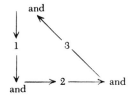

c.   The Four beat   Four divided

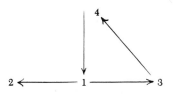   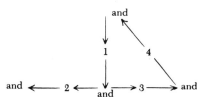

d. The Five beat:

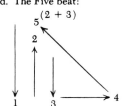   *or*   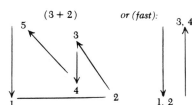   *or (fast):*      *or*

e. The Six beat

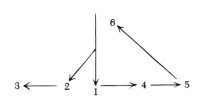   *or (fast):*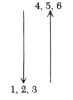

To be used sparingly, but of value in ritards of the basic 2 and 3 beat. Usually a divided 2 results in a 4 pattern and a divided 3 in a 6 pattern.

f. The Seven beat

(4 + 3) 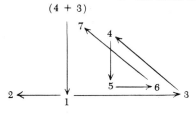   or: (3 + 4) 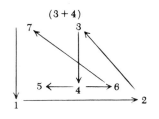   or (fast): (2 + 2 + 3)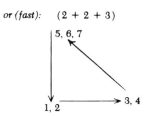

or: (3 + 2 + 2) 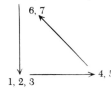   or: (2 + 3 + 2)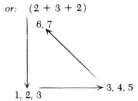

g. The Eight beat

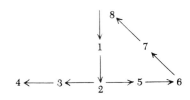

h. The Nine beat

or (fast):

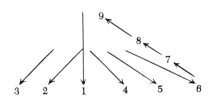 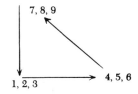

i. The Ten beat and the Eleven beat

These two patterns should be practiced in the following combinations:

1. 2+3+3+2; 3+2+2+3; 4+4+2; 4+2+4
2. 3+3+3+2; 4+4+3; or any combination of these

j. The Twelve beat

or (fast):

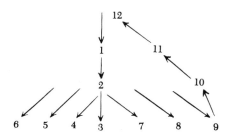 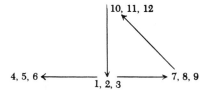

k. The One beat

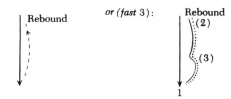

2. The Two, Three, Four beats with connecting "loops" to be applied to all patterns:

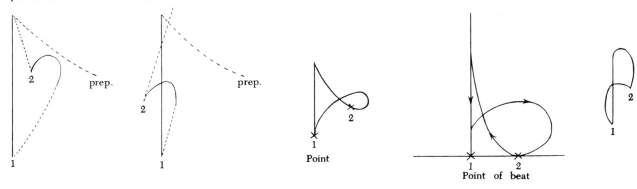

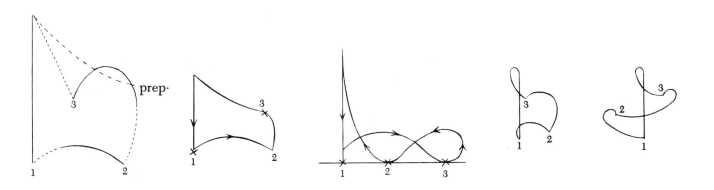

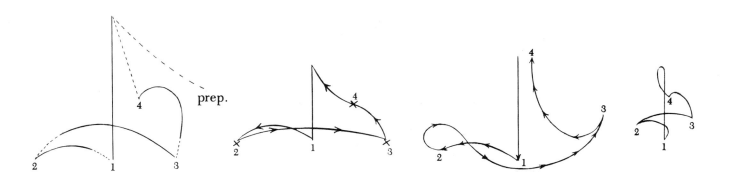

The shape of the beat

There are two fundamental gestures used in conducting and these correspond to the two elementary opposites in music: legato and staccato. A legato line should be indicated by a longer drawn-out movement while the staccato should be executed by a quick, jagged stroke. No one could hope to list all the variations of the loops and the expressive "taffy pulling" as Koussevitsky used to call it. However, the shape of the beat pattern will immediately communicate the style and the form of expression to the chorus or to the accompaniment if present.

Another most important aspect of the shape of the beat is the "point" or the "stopping bounce" of each stroke. Too many conductors have a "swimming" beat which revolves constantly without a stop so that one stroke runs into another without definition. This causes confusion and inarticulate rhythms, and certainly does not engender a more expressive performance no matter how pleading the gestures may be. The best results are obtained when the "point" of a beat is executed as if a weight were being dropped, then as though it rebounded slightly to form a loop to the next beat. The deliberateness or the caressing quality of the "drop" of the beat should of course be determined by the kind of expressive quality sought. In other words, a pointed, almost "stopped," beat means staccato, while a very sensitive looping gesture will indicate a more legato line. Gradations of each should be practiced on all beat patterns, and the graphs on pages 11—13 studied for additional ideas.

The "preparation," "preliminary" or "warning" beat

This is one of the most important lessons to learn and one of primary importance since the decisiveness and the character of this preparatory gesture determines the exactness of attack as well as the tempo, dynamics, and expressive character of the opening of the ensuing work. The preparation beat should therefore have the duration that is the length and character of the first beat of the first measure. The conductor should inhale to this beat, and this must signify to the chorus the moment to inhale also. If this coordination is well affected, it establishes an immediate rapport between conductor and choir, and the more naturally the preparatory beat and the inhaling can be carried off the greater will be the precision and the decisiveness of the beginning. There are three kinds of "warning" or preparatory beats: one to prepare an entrance of a piece which begins on the beat; one where a full rest occurs before the entrance (or a full upbeat); and a third preparation beat which prepares for an entrance occurring between two beats.

Examples:

a.

Preparation beat on 3 of "previous" measure.

b.

Preparation beat on the "second" beat, the beat before the upbeat.

c.

Preparation beat on the first eighth or the strong part of this broken beat should be especially decisive and strongly indicated as a preparatory gesture. No problem should then ensue. However, to ensure a substantial and rhythmic eighth-note upbeat the eyes should be used, or if absolutely necessary a subdivision of the beat should be affected by means of a slight wrist motion.

The release

Similarly the closing gesture or "cutoff" must be carefully studied. When the final note of the piece is held, the release sign is usually made in one of three ways, although there are others:

1. The conductor moves his hand to the left on the last beat of the held note to notify the chorus that the "cutoff" is about to follow, and immediately thereafter makes a sweeping gesture to the right or a downward gesture resembling a downbeat to signify the actual release.

2. He reverses the direction of the warning sign, moving to the right with the sweep gesture going to the left.

3. Some conductors open their hands for the warning sign and close them for the actual cutoff. This is especially effective when the last word ends with a consonant and it ensures uniform execution of sounds like "t," "s," as well as "m," and "n."

The cutoff must not be unprepared or overly sudden; otherwise members of the group may complain that such a sudden gesture makes them feel as if they were going to "bite their tongues."

4. One special problem must be discussed before the subject of the cutoff: the fermata or hold. There are four types of fermatas.

    a. A hold at the end of a composition.

    b. A fermata that is *not* followed by any kind of silence or caesura.

    c. A hold that is followed by a short, unmeasured period of silence. It is sometimes indicated by a *luftpause* sign, or a phrase fermata of the type found in a Bach chorale.

    d. A fermata followed by a long measured or unmeasured pause.

The first type is rather a simple problem: For the concluding fermata, regardless of the note value over which it appears, beat only one count, hold it as long as you feel it should be held, and end it with a simple cutoff motion. One piece of advice may be helpful. If the conductor does not give specific indications, a fermata can undercut the effectiveness of the dynamics by destroying the rhythmic intensity. For this reason, it is suggested that the raising of either hand to signify continued forte, or even crescendo or fortissimo, will give a more vital sound and dynamic range to the note or chord which is held. Conversely, the lowering of the hand before the cutoff has the effect of piano, diminuendo, or morendo.

Exercises for this type of "final" fermata:

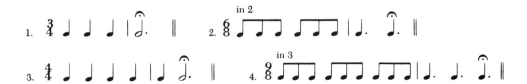

The second kind of hold should be conducted by holding the beat at the "bounce" point, of the gesture and then proceeding to the next beat in the traditional manner, without a cutoff after the hold.

Exercises:

The third type of fermata should also be held at the "bounce" point. If the silence is just a short *luftpause*, it is best to utilize the cutoff of the fermata as the preparation beat for the next beat. In other words, the length of the interruption is shown by the length of time the conductor pauses between the cutoff and the "bounce" point of the next measured or strictly metered beat.

Exercises:

The fourth and final kind of fermata included in our discussion, is very closely related to the third; the only difference being that the silence is longer. Once again the cutoff of the hold should signify the beginning of the pause; in this case, however, the hands should be motionless after the cutoff sign and remain so for as long as the conductor desires the interruption to last. Then he should resume the beating as if he were commencing a new piece by indicating a preparatory beat preceding the next sung beat.

Exercises:

The fourth type of fermata is often used for very dramatic effects. All fermatas and caesuras depend on the musical judgment and taste of the individual conductor, as well as his knowledge of the particular stylistic practices of any creative period of the past and present. It is strongly urged that the student read a great deal of supplementary material on this subject in the conducting books by Scherchen, Weingartner, Rudolf, Green, McElheran, Thomas and Garretson.[2]

Size of the beat

The size of the beat should be in direct proportion to the loudness or softness of the music. A small beat should be used for piano passages making sure that if there is a pianissimo marking, the beat can become even smaller. The converse is true for the gestures dealing with louder music. This leads to a word about silences. The student should be urged to conduct rests as well as notes, for nothing destroys the continuity and rhythmic structure of a work more than the sloppy, ad libitum handling of pauses by many conductors. Of course unmeasured pauses such as may be designated by fermatas are an exception to this rule. There is such a thing as "dynamic silence" to borrow a term from John Cage, and even though a smaller gesture should be used when all are resting, the beat must be continued.

Visual Contact

Even though visual contact is an aspect of conducting that is not directly concerned with right-hand technique or with the mechanics of the left hand, it must be mentioned at the outset, for it is possibly the most crucial factor governing all of conducting. It goes without saying that the conductor should have eye contact with all singers at the preliminary beat, the first beats of the piece, again at the warning gesture for the "cutoff," and at the closing signal. More than during these obvious times, the conductor must know his score so well that his eyes are upon his singers, and if need be on his accompanying group most of the time during performance as well as during rehearsal. While conducting from memory is certainly not a prerequisite for a good performance, a knowledge of each part, and of the consummate music resulting from the sum of these parts is essential. While conducting the examples in the first three chapters, the eyes should be used to aid the right hand without resorting to the left hand for help, especially for denoting entrances, to express dynamic changes, as well as to signal important tempo or rhythmic variations. Many outstanding conductors achieve their greatest results by means of the visual contact they maintain with their musicians during an entire performance. An expressive eye must be conscientiously trained and vigorously cultivated along with a naturalness in executing beat patterns.

At the beginning of these first exercises every student should study each example whether assigned to conduct it or not. This preparation will enable him to criticize his fellow student more constructively when the

[2] *Handbook of Conducting* by Herman Scherchen, Oxford University Press, London, 1942. *Weingartner on Music and Conducting*, Three Essays by Felix Weingartner, New York: Dover Publications, 1969. *The Grammar of Conducting* by Max Rudolf, New York: G. Schirmer, 1950. *The Modern Conductor* by Elizabeth A. H. Green, Englewood Cliffs, N.J.: Prentice-Hall, 1969. *Conducting Technique* by Brock McElheran, New York: Oxford University Press, 1966. *Lehrbuch der Chorleitung* by Kurt Thomas, Breitkopf und Härtel, Wiesbaden, English translation, New York: Associated Music Publishers, 1968. *Conducting Choral Music* by Robert L. Garretson, Boston: Allyn and Bacon, 1965.

class performance leads to a class critique. In laying the ground rules for the most effective use of this anthology, it is urged that the conditions and attitudes of performance should simulate those most commonly encountered by a choral conductor, in other words, members of the class should consider themselves a practicing chorus. Then, when it is the student's turn to conduct, he should remember two things:

a. The object of mastering technique in an art is to achieve a desired end with the greatest simplicity and economy of means. Do not talk too much—communicate musically!

b. The conductor's use of gymnastics and overt distracting gesticulations—mostly employed for the enjoyment of the audience—are objectionable. The stiff, passive, impersonal, unexcitable and dull conductor is, however, equally undesirable and cannot bring about a good performance. The student should remember that the inner beat or the feeling of faster units within a longer note adds intensity and urgency to the movement of the music. Practice, for instance, conducting a slow $\frac{4}{4}$ pattern, feeling triplets during each gesture; then four-sixteenths to the beat. Feel the impact on your entire body and cultivate this kind of inner beat excitement, whether the music is fast or slow, and you will always have a vital performance. Remember the analogy once given by Archibald T. Davison: conducting a choir is like throwing a rubber ball at a stone wall; "There is as much rebound as there is force in the throw."

ALLELUIA, HAEC DIES
Ignazio Donati

This early seventeenth-century motet may be performed with or without the violin part, however it does add an extra yet unessential line above the interplay of the voices. The spirit is exuberant, and the dynamics as they are printed here, should be observed throughout. Ignazio Donati was an Italian composer who published eight books of church sonatas and seven books of motets, masses, and psalms.

HOLIDAY SONG
William Schuman
Words by Genevieve Taggard

The "Holiday Song" by William Schuman, with words by Genevieve Taggard, was published in 1942. The excerpt given here, measures 29 through 49, is a kind of refrain and stands in the middle of this very popular choral work. The piano accompaniment is essential.

16

LIEBESLIEDER WALZER
Opus 52, No. 8

Johannes Brahms

Edited by Robert Shaw. Text from Polydora, by von Daumer.
English translation by Basil Swift.

This is the eighth of the Liebeslieder (Love Song) Walzer. It should be conducted in a rather slow one beat in order to have the "Viennese lilt" and yet not rush. Take all the repeats and be sure that the dynamics are even softer the second time the piece is performed. If the left hand of the second piano gives a staccato articulation to the first beat of the measure, the effect of "lilting" will be greatly aided. Do not try to beat this in three, for it will give the piece a heavy feeling that is definitely out of style and most undesirable.

hold me, Ev - 'ry care and trou - ble flees,____ as your love en - folds____ me;
schau - et, je - de letz - te Trü - be flieht,____ wel - che mich um - grau ____ et.

hold me, Ev - 'ry care and trou - ble flees,____ as your love en - folds me;
schau - et, je - de letz - te Trü - be flieht,____ wel - che mich um - grau ~ et.

hold me, Ev - 'ry care and trou - ble flees,____ as your love en - folds____ me;
schau - et, je - de letz - te Trü - be flieht,____ wel - che mich um - grau ~ et.

hold me, Ev - 'ry care and trou - ble flees, as your love en - folds me;
schau - et, je - de letz - te Trü - be flieht, wel - che mich um - grau ~ et.

I

II

'Tis a sweet - ly burn - ing flame, Leave it not____ un -
Die - ser Lie - be schö - ne Glut,____ lass sie nicht____ ver -

'Tis a sweet - ly burn - ing flame,____ Leave it not____ un -
Die - ser Lie - be schö ~ ~ ~ ne Glut,____ lass sie nicht____ ver -

'Tis a sweet - ly burn - ing flame,____ Leave it not un - ten ~ ~
Die - ser Lie - be schö ~ ne Glut,____ lass sie nicht ver - stie ~ ~

'Tis a sweet - ly burn - ing flame, Leave it not un - ten ~ ~
Die - ser Lie - be schö ~ ne Glut, lass sie nicht ver - stie ~ ~

I

II

MORNING
(*Morgen*)

György Ligeti

After a poem by Sandor Weöres
Free English version by György Ligeti

Here is an excerpt from the second of two a cappella choruses written in 1955 by the famous Hungarian composer György Ligeti. It is not an example of his later style, for he is best known for such works as "Atmospheres," the "Lux Aeterna" from his *Requiem,* and "Adventure." These two light madrigals are proof of his great compositional skill even in a tonal idiom, and because of their effectiveness as choral pieces should be programmed much more often. It is suggested that the excerpt be practiced rather slowly at first, then increased in speed as the chorus learns the pitches, and finally at full speed ♩ = 184. However, it is strongly urged that even at a slower tempo the piece always be conducted in one so that everyone will learn to feel it that way. Perhaps a rolled "R" on the word "Ring" will give a more vital first accent throughout, and care must be taken to use the beginning consonants to keep the piece sprightly.

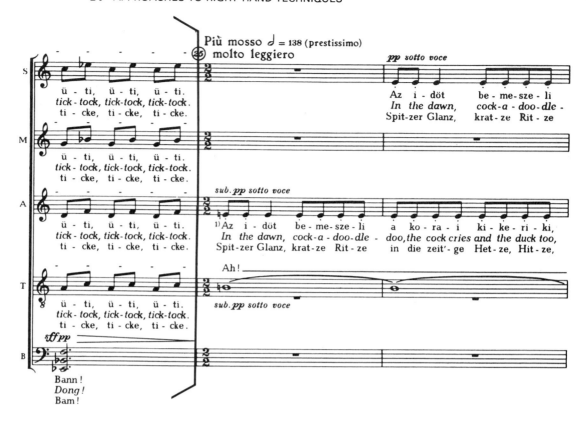

BEHOLD, MY SAVIOUR NOW IS TAKEN
From *St. Matthew Passion*

Johann Sebastian Bach

Many of the choruses from Bach's Passions have the "bite" of agony and terror. This one is typical of that genre. It is difficult to perform, not only because of its speed and contrapuntal complexities, but also because care must be taken that the separate eighth notes are performed staccato, while the sixteenth-note runs come out smoothly and evenly. While the tempo should be in one as fast as possible, there must be spaces in between the staccato eighth notes so that the steadiness is not disturbed by rushing these "shortened" notes.

JACK DER SPRATT

From *Songs Mein Grossmama Sang*

Music by Lloyd Pfautsch

Words by David Morrah

"Jack der Spratt" is a fun song for three part chorus from a short collection of choruses called *Songs Mein Grossmama Sang*, by Lloyd Pfautsch. The independent accompaniment has its own rhythmic figures that makes this a bit tricky to conduct. However, a good "beat bounce" will take care of all the difficulties. At first perhaps an entire measure of preparation may be helpful in establishing both the rhythm and the mood. Do not resort to conducting in 3, where a note is placed on the second or last beat of a measure, unless it is absolutely necessary.

O VOS OMNES QUI TRANSISTIS PER VIAM

From *Lamentations of Jeremiah*

Alberto Ginastera

These are the first 49 bars of the *Lamentations* by the distinguished Argentinian composer, Alberto Ginastera. The grace notes are on the beat and the voices overlap without a break. The rhythm should be steady, especially in the tenor and bass parts of measures 10–14, and throughout the fugue.

*Para ensayos solamente
For rehearsal only

A JUBILANT SONG
Norman Dello Joio

Words adapted from Walt Whitman

It has been demonstrated that the "one beat" may contain three or two counts, but here we have an excerpt that is to be conducted in one, yet it contains five eighth notes in each stroke. Every student in the class should try this exercise because the "feeling" of each of these measures is unique. One must at first consciously count to five so that one does not "rob" each measure by cutting the final quarter note and making it an eighth, or "fatten" it by making that note a dotted quarter. The piano has the chance of establishing the beat quite solidly by the time the chorus enters, and the conductor should use this opportunity to conduct each of the measures during the piano opening as well as during the interlude to keep everything stable.

KYRIE

From *Missa Iste Confessor*

Giovanni Pierluigi Da Palestrina

Revised and organ score arranged by Herbert Zipper

The thematic basis for this mass is the melody of the Gregorian hymn, "Iste Confessor" (eighth mode). It was published by Palestrina in 1590 in his fifth book of masses. This arrangement raises the entire work a whole tone, because the tessitura of the alto part is inconveniently low. The small accidentals over the notes are supplied by the editor: the ones printed in front of the notes were contained in the original manuscript. It would be advisable to use only the boldly printed ones (both within and outside the parentheses) in order to maintain the intended modal idiom.

* The "ei" in "eleison" is a diphthong; therefore the "i" has to be slurred to the preceding "e". The change from "e" to "i" on a whole note or half note comes at the last moment before "son".

* **Here and in all subsequent analogous places, doubled octaves to be played only on the Piano.**

IL EST BEL ET BON?
Passereau

The composer of this very popular chanson is known only by his last name. Not much is known about his life except that he lived during the early part of the sixteenth century, was a chapel-singer for the Duke of Angonlême, and published 23 chansons in various collections between 1533 and 1547. This, the best known of his works, is really a kind of musical joke. Two farm wives are discussing the husband of one of them, saying, "He is handsome and good, he does not get angry, nor does he beat me, and while he feeds the chickens, I am having a good time. Is that not a handsome and good man?" The tempo of the piece should be very rapid, and the reason this edition was used was because it gives no expression marks. The conductor must choose. To simulate the two gossiping wives, it is suggested the chanson be sung pianissimo throughout, making sure that it is fluid and smooth without any accents, and certainly as if there were no bar lines.

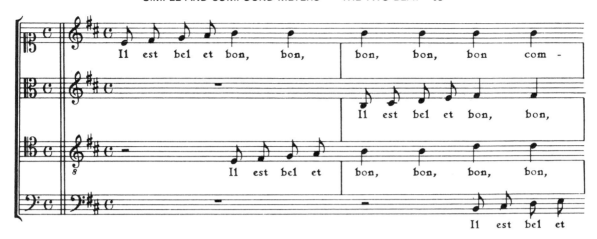

NOW, O NOW I NEEDS MUST PART

John Dowland

A typical English Madrigal by John Dowland, one of the greatest English composers of the sixteenth century. Each gesture of the two beat must feel as if it contained three quarter notes. Even though there is some sadness in the text, do not take it too seriously and do not perform this madrigal in a morose manner. Keep it light. A good tempo may be ♩. = 76.

Deutsche Textunterlegung: E.K.

THE CRICKET
(*El Grillo*)

Josquin des Préz

Adapted and translated by Marlin Merrill

A Belgian by birth, Josquin des Préz spent over thirty years of his life in Italy. This charming "frottola" which imitates the chirping of a cricket shows an Italian influence. The frottola was the leading Italian form of the sixteenth century and was the predecessor of the madrigal. It would be advisable to leave out the "editorial" natural signs in front of the G flat, and make the tempo about 120 to 126 to the half note.

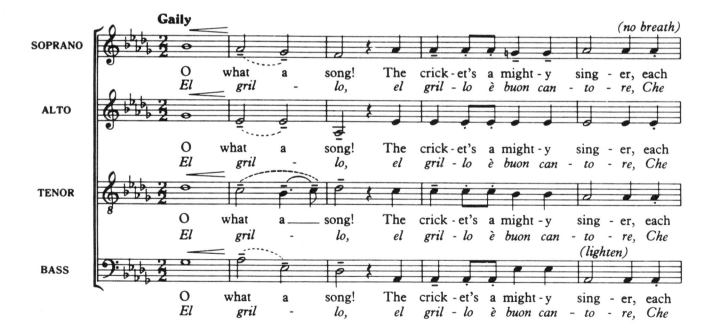

Note: accidentals printed small are editorial.

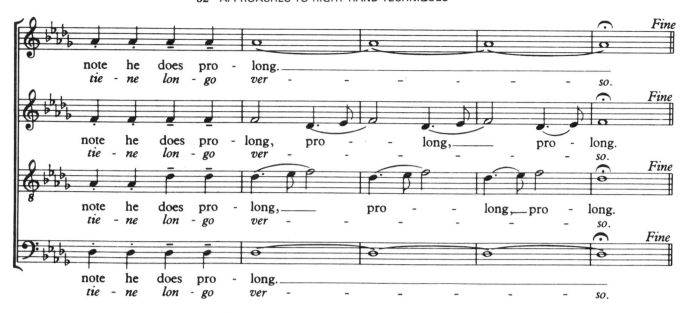

ve - ry pret - ty,   ve - ry,   ve - ry   pret - ty sings the crick - et!
dal - le, dal - le, be - ve, be - ve, gril - lo, gril - lo can - ta!

ve - ry pret - ty,   ve - ry,   ve - ry   pret - ty sings the crick - et!
dal - le, dal - le, be - ve, be - ve, gril - lo, gril - lo can - ta!

ve - ry pret - ty,   ve - ry,   ve - ry   pret - ty sings the crick - et!
dal - le, dal - le, be - ve, be - ve, gril - lo, gril - lo can - ta!

ve - ry pret - ty,   ve - ry,   ve - ry   pret - ty sings the crick - et!
dal - le, dal - le, be - ve, be - ve, gril - lo, gril - lo can - ta!

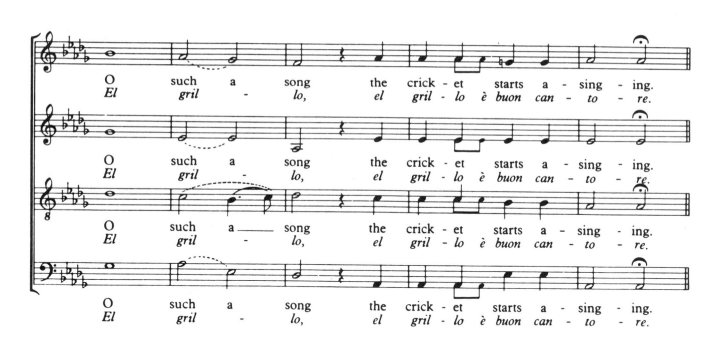

O   such   a   song   the crick - et starts a - sing - ing.
El   gril - lo,   el gril - lo è buon can - to - re.

O   such   a   song   the crick - et starts a - sing - ing.
El   gril - lo,   el gril - lo è buon can - to - re.

O   such   a ___ song   the crick - et starts a - sing - ing.
El   gril - lo,   el gril - lo è buon can - to - re.

O   such   a   song   the crick - et starts a - sing - ing.
El   gril - lo,   el gril - lo è buon can - to - re.

3 ROUNDS IN $\frac{6}{8}$ TIME

    The singing of rounds and catches has been a favorite pastime for centuries. During the eighteenth century several clubs in England called the Noblemen and Gentlemen's Catch Clubs held competitions both for the creation and the performance of canons and catches. Even today it is refreshing to program a round or series of rounds as part of a choral concert. Further, it is excellent training for the chorus to be exposed to singing "equal" parts at different times, a practice that develops the ear of the performers. This first set of rounds in this volume should challenge the conductor in several ways: first, to keep a steady tempo; second, to give clear and correct entrances to each voice; third, to handle the *fermata* in the first round; fourth, to supply dynamics, which are not given, but are left to the conductor. In "Kiss and Tell" there is an obvious "stylistic mistake," since parallel 5ths occur in the first two parts between measures 6 and 7 and again between 8 and 9. It is rather charming, but a bit "out of style"; therefore, the middle voice could substitute a "g" instead of a "d" as the final pitch of measures 6 and 8. The third of the three $\frac{6}{8}$ rounds, "The Interrupted Assignation," is especially choice since it was written by one of the great British masters of the eighteenth century.

Mr. Speaker

Joseph Baildon

-bate,   I   must length — — — en the de - bate,   Mis - ter

stir,   if you stir,   Sir, I shall name you if you stir,   Sir, I shall

chair,   pray sup - port the chair,   pray sup - port the   chair.   Ques - tion,

To 2

Speaker, tho' 'tis late,   I   must lengthen the _ de - bate.

To 3

name you, Sir, I shall name you, Sir, I shall name you if you stir.

To 1

Or - der, hear him, hear,   pray sup - port, sup-port _ the chair.

Kiss and Tell

Lord Mornington

The Interrupted Assignation

Thomas Arne

this;   No coy-ness —   come, kiss me,   Oh, further my

What are y'a-bout?   For shame!   Now I hate you,   I

head!   A-gain!   And a-gain!   'Tis the creak of the

bliss,   fur-ther,   fur-ther,   oh,   further, oh, further my

vow   I'll   cry   mur-der!   mur-der!   I   vow, I vow I'll cry

bed,   a-gain,   and a-gain,   'tis the creak of the bed, the creak of the

bliss.   The old wo-man's lame;   we have

out.   Hark!   Hark!   Ma-dam calls —

bed.   Jen-ny!   (A plague o' this gout —   Oh!

no-thing,   no-thing to   dread;   I'm dy-ing,   I'm

Lud!   What shall I   do?   I'm coming,   I'm

I'm rea-dy to   swoon.) Why, Jenny, _____   Jen-ny, _____

dy-ing,   nay, now,   now I am   dead.   To 2

coming,   and John,   John's coming too.   To 3

_____   why John,   this   minute, this minute come   down.   To 1

YVER, VOUS N'ESTES QU'UN VILLAIN
From *Trois Chansons*

Claude Debussy

Words by Charles D'Orleans; English words by Nita Cox

The *Trois Chansons* by Claude Debussy are among the great treasury of a cappella choral music of the early twentieth century. The impressionistic French master did not write a great deal of a cappella choral music, but these three chansons are certainly worthy of attention and would be gems to program on any concert. Unlike madrigals, chansons, and part songs of earlier periods that often leave the expression marks to the discretion of the interpreter or more frequently to an editor, Debussy clearly marks his intentions on every phrase, if not every note. These dynamics and phrasings must be observed literally in order to obtain the best performance results. Notice that the composer often asks for contrasting articulations simultaneously (measures 15–18). This presents a real challenge to the conductor, and the left hand should come into play showing the lower voices' *legato* lines while the *staccato* is being negotiated by the soprano. It may be well to work on this piece again after studying chapter 5.

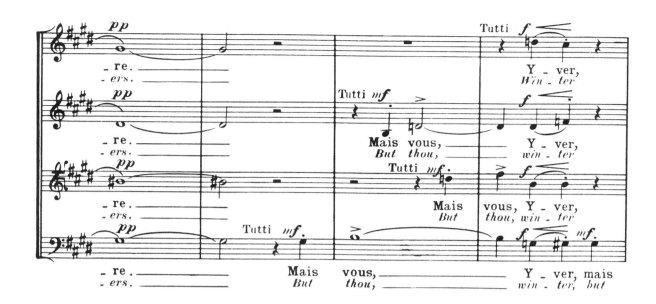

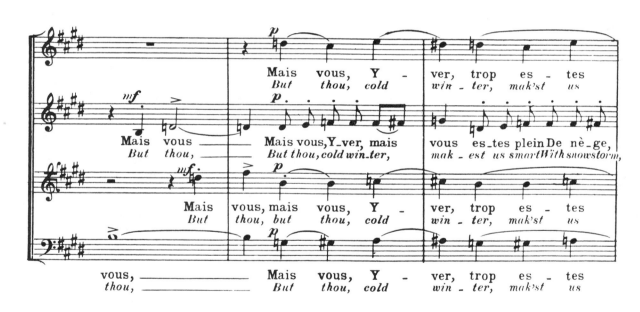

TE DEUM
Vincent Persichetti

An excerpt from the *Te Deum* by Vincent Persichetti, Opus 93, published in 1964. Follow the dynamics carefully and keep the eighth notes flowing evenly. Be sure that the piano plays the ''marcato'' notes strongly accented against the smooth lines of the other parts; the half note entrances should be beautiful and precise but unaccented.

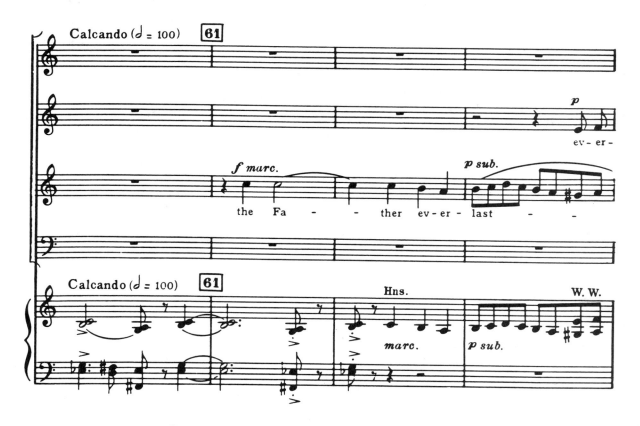

WAVE ALL THE FLAGS IN THE COUNTRY
(*Werfet Panier Auf Im Lande*)

Georg Philipp Telemann
English version by Joseph Boonin

Edited by Abraham Kaplan

This rousing and spirited motet by G. P. Telemann should present no conductorial problems if the beat is clearly delineated, and the dotted eight note is perfectly proportioned. Use the consonants to provide natural accents. This gives a wonderful feeling and lift to the music.

SINCE ALL IS PASSING
From *Six Chansons*

Paul Hindemith

Original French poem by Rainer Maria Rilke
English version by Elaine de Sinçay

The first of two pages of the third "Chanson" in a group of six by Paul Hindemith. *Six Chansons* has become a very popular work for choral performances and is perhaps a contemporary classic. The beat should be very small, expressing the inherent "fleeting" quality. Do not overemphasize the crescendo and diminuendo of the third and fourth measures, and keep any climax in reserve for the next part of the piece.

FIRE, FIRE, MY HEART
Thomas Morley

Edited and arranged by Noble Cain

This must be one of the most performed madrigals in the entire repertoire, and for good reason. It includes all the elements of the characteristic British sixteenth-century art form. Here is a joyous, rhythmically exciting piece with many "fa la la's," and at the same time the "cry for help" and its ensuing pathos created by the composer's setting of the words. Once again, as for most music of this period, the dynamic markings are purely editorial, and certainly the crescendo and diminuendo marks at "but none comes high" should not be slavishly followed. All the markings are only suggestions to recreate the mood of the words and music most effectively. It is certainly not clear from the spacing of the chord at the words, "Ah me!" whether the composer meant such a *subito* pp. This kind of grief could also be expressed in a loud fashion. In order to find the best solution concerning dynamics in this madrigal, it would be best to assign it to several conductors, each experimenting with a different set of dynamics.

me, and call for help, a - las!___ but none comes

and ___ call for help, a-las! but none

me, and call___ for help, a - las! but none come nigh me, but

me, and call for help, a - las! a-las! but

call for help, a - las! but none comes nigh me, but none comes

nigh me! Fa la la la la la la,

___comes nigh___ me! Fa la

none comes nigh me! Fa___ la la la la la la la la, fa la

none comes nigh me! Fa la la la la la la la la, fa la la la

nigh me! Fa la la la la la la la la la la,

ALLELUIA
From *Brazilian Psalm*

Jean Berger
Words by Jorge de Lima

This is an excerpt from the first movement of Jean Berger's *Brazilian Psalm.* Syncopation and entrances off the beat are the problems here. The conducting motion should be kept small enough to maintain the subtle dynamics, but firm and rhythmic enough to give the syncopated "bounce." The soprano descant line should be very smooth and quite independent. About ♩ = 88.

lu - ia,   al - le - lu - ia, al - le - lu - ia, al - le - lu - ia,   al - le -
lu - ia,   al - le - lu - ia, al - le-lu-ia, al - le - lu - ia,   al - le -
al - le - lu-ia, al - le-lu-ia,   al - le - lu - ia,   al - le-lu - ia, al - le-lu - ia,
al - le - lu-ia, al - le - lu-ia,   al - le - lu - ia,

lu - ia, al - le - lu - ia, al - le - lu - ia,   al - le -
lu - ia, al - le - lu - ia, al - le - lu - ia,   al - le -
al - le - lu - ia,   al - le - lu - ia, al - le - lu - ia,
al - le - lu - ia,   al - le - lu - ia,

lu - ia, al - le - lu - ia, al - le - lu - ia,   al - le -
lu - ia, al - le - lu - ia, al - le - lu - ia,   al - le -
al - le - lu - ia,   al - le - lu - ia, al -
al - le - lu - ia,   al - le - lu - ia, al -

VENI SANCTE SPIRITUS
Peter Maxwell Davies

Measures 76–85 of Peter Maxwell Davies' twenty-minute motet *Veni Sancte Spiritus*, written in 1963. Here the conductor must constantly feel 3 beats against 2. It is a very difficult excerpt, but important to master because there are many such passages in twentieth-century literature. Work on this piece slowly at first, and give a measure of 2 beats before you begin. Then build up your proficiency until the piece can be performed at the required speed: Allegro molto ♩ = 152. (Begin at the arrow.)

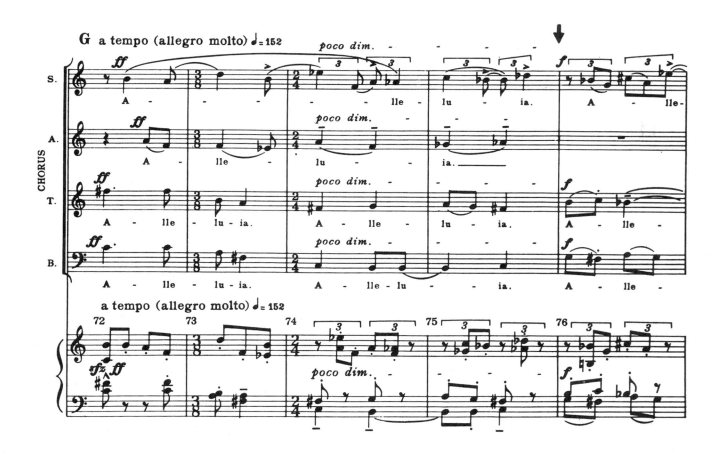

3 ROUNDS IN $\frac{3}{4}$ TIME

In this second set of rounds, we have two written by William Horsley (1774–1858) and one by Samuel Webbe (1740–1816). Both composers were active in the Catch Club movement in England. Webbe, who was born in Minorca, won 27 medals in as many years for his outstanding contributions to the repertory of the Catch Club. He was mostly a composer of secular music, but at the same time served as organist of the Sardinian Embassy Chapel in London. It is said that he was one of the most important secular choral composers of his generation. A worthwhile project might be to research some of these composers' choral music, especially since Horsley was a friend of Mendelssohn's and was held in great esteem by the German master. Horsley also edited Byrd's "Cantiones Sacrae" for the British Antiquarian Society and was one of the co-founders of the Philharmonic Society of London in 1813. The conductor should read the words of each round carefully to decide the appropriate tempo and dynamics for their most satisfactory interpretation.

Sweet Are the Blushes

William Horsley
Words by Drummond of Hawthornden

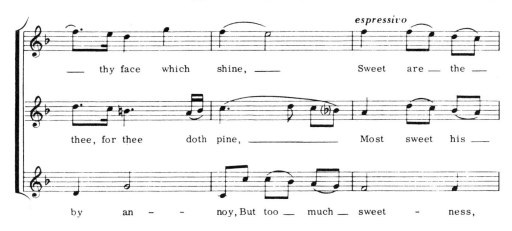

_____ thy face   which   shine, _____   Sweet   are _ the _

thee, for thee   doth   pine, _____   Most   sweet   his _

by   an - - noy, But too _ much _ sweet - ness,

flames   which sparkle   from _____   thy   eyes. _ | Sweet _   To 2

death,   for thee   who sweet-ly, sweet-ly   dies. _ | To 3

too much sweetness and a - bun - dant   joy. | To 1

(End here.)

Stay, Daphne, Stay

Samuel Webbe

A Pastoral

William Horsley

PROVERB
Vincent Persichetti

"Proverb" by Vincent Persichetti is a very simple choral piece which confronts one with the "upbeat" question. After utilizing the piano for the first few times, try this a cappella; you should be able to detect any pitch discrepancies in this rather uncomplicated melodic and harmonic style.

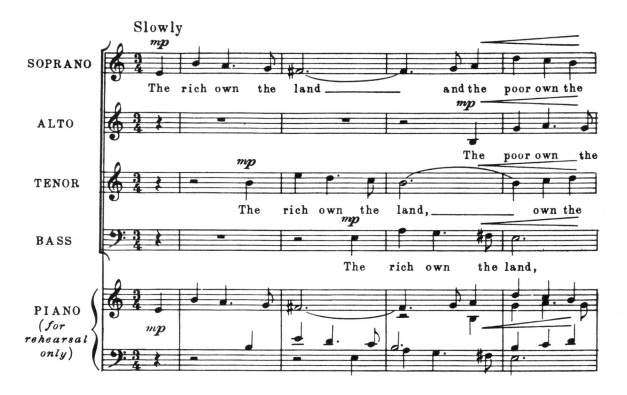

THE LAMB
From *The Wondrous Kingdom*

Mark Bucci

Here we have the third chorus of a cycle of nine by Mark Bucci, titled *The Wonderous Kingdom*; it was published in 1958. In keeping with the childlike character of the poem, the composer has set the words in a very straight-forward manner. Build the phrases slowly, and closely observe the dynamic markings.

WHERE WILT THOU

From *St. Matthew Passion*

Johann Sebastian Bach

"Where Wilt Thou" is one of the many short but very powerful choruses from Bach's *St. Matthew Passion*. Make certain that the entrances of the chorus in the beginning absolutely coincide with the accompaniment, and that the effect of the question is poignant and comes through in the performance.

14 Chorus

Chorus I

WHEN JESUS WEPT

Music by William Billings

Edited by Clarence Dickinson

From *The New England Psalm Singer*, 1770

William Billings is one of the earliest American composers about whom we have any information. He was born in Boston in 1746 and died in 1800. "When Jesus Wept" is one of his "fuguing tunes"; it has a strange archaic flavor and a great deal of charm. The dynamic marks are supplied by the editor; but it stands to reason that Billings intended a crescendo each time the tune is presented. ♩ = 60 is an appropriate speed.

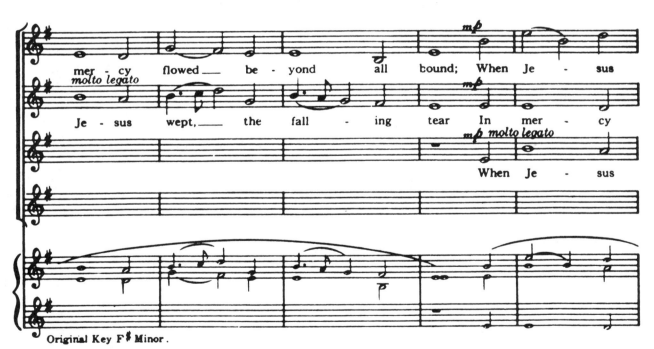

Original Key F# Minor.

This round may be sung by any combination of voices: four women's voices; four men's voices; or S.A.T.B. When men's voices are used, it may be desirable to transpose the round down a tone to D minor.

THE SHEPHERDS' FAREWELL TO THE HOLY FAMILY
From *L'Enfance du Christ*

Hector Berlioz

A very "Christmasy" excerpt from *L'Enfance du Christ* written by Hector Berlioz in 1854 as a religious trilogy for soli, chorus, and orchestra. It is a strophic piece set off by a beautiful, simple, four-measure introduction. Handle the piece as if it were an uncomplicated Christmas Carol, with strict adherence to the dynamic markings. After performing it, one should listen to the orchestration. Metronome marking ♪ = 112.

PSALM 148
Gustav Holst

In this setting of the 148th Psalm by Gustav Holst, the hymnlike beginning leads to jubilation on the word "Alleluia." Follow the dynamics closely in order to prevent the early build-ups from lessening the tremendous climax, which occurs later on. The traditional German seventeenth-century melody "Ye Watchers and Ye Holy Ones" provides the basis for this work. $\quad \downarrow = 69$.

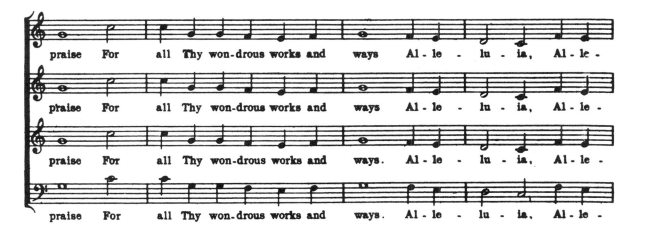

SANCTUS

From *Missa Pange Lingua*

Josquin des Préz

This is an excerpt from Josquin des Préz' very famous Mass, *Missa Pange Lingua.* The tempo should be rather slow; the whole note at 60 would be a reasonable speed to sustain the dignity and keep it moving. Let the line determine the dynamics naturally, begin each voice at piano and in measure 12 reach forte. Watch the notation; remembering that the bar lines are only for the convenience of the conductor, and the dotted whole note at the end of measure 13 extends into the next measure.

OMNES GENTES
Gordon Binkerd

The first 15 measures of a long motet, *Omnes Gentes*, by Gordon Binkerd. This music should be handled gently and encouraged to flow freely and peacefully. After mentally feeling 3 to every beat, the conductor must make sure that the duplets in measures 12–13 occupy the same space as the three eighth notes did up to measure 12.

LAUDATE DOMINUM, NO. 1
From *Cinque Laude*

Norman Dinerstein

The first of five "Laude" by Norman Dinerstein. The soprano and alto sing music of a similar nature; the tenor and bass are quite independent. The grace notes should be on the beat so a strong second beat is required. Make sure that the composer's wish for sf-p in the bass is observed. Build the crescendo carefully, not too quickly, and remember the subito piano at measure 7.

I.

Stagger breathing when necessary.

THREE DESCANTS

No. 1

From *Ecclesiastes*

Karl Kohn

The first few pages of Karl Kohn's "Descants" require very sustained lines. Be certain that the eighth rests are observed at the beginning and the dotted eighth-sixteenth figure has vibrancy. The dynamics and the accompaniment are most important. The abrupt cutoff at the end of the excerpt is in the music; only the chord is held, and a new phrase begins. Be careful of the intonation throughout.

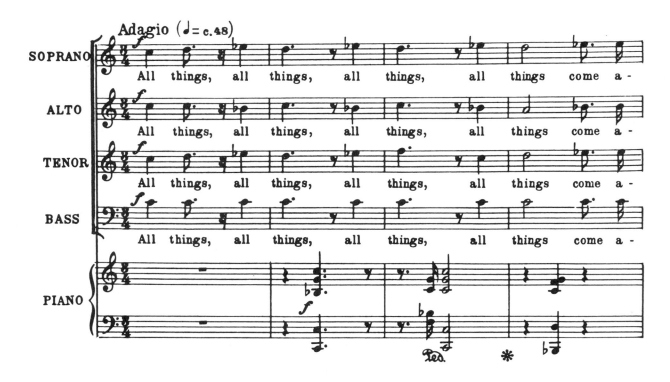

TWO CHORALES

Johann Sebastian Bach

These two chorales by J. S. Bach should lead to a discussion of phrasing and the fermata (hold) after each phrase. More recently, we have dispensed with the stops after each short phrase and have decided to combine and elongate them. In the "Jesu, Priceless Treasure," the author would suggest a continuous phrase until after "to me," succeeded by another terminating in "for Thee," followed, without further interruption, by a build to the end. It is probable that the stops were important when these chorales were sung by congregations; however, both the melody and the harmony provide a natural cadence which make the fermata and a complete stop unnecessary. It would be advisable for students to do further research on this subject.

(A) "Jesu, Priceless Treasure"

(B) "Break Forth, O Beauteous Heavenly Light"

Break forth, O beau-teous heaven-ly light, And ush - er in the morn - ing;
Ye shep - herds, shrink not with af - fright, But hear the an - gels warn - ing.

This child, now weak in in - fan - cy, Our con - fi - dence and joy shall be, The

power of Sa - tan break - ing, Our peace e - ter - nal mak - ing.

APRIL IS IN MY MISTRESS' FACE

From *Invitation to Madrigals, Book 2, for SATB,* Edited by Thurston Dart

Thomas Morley

The true English madrigal was created almost single-handedly by Thomas Morley (1558–1602?), who wrote a series of books containing madrigals, canzonets, and so on, and published them between 1593–1597. "April Is in My Mistress' Face" is one of Morley's most famous madrigals, and is part of a collection bearing the date 1594. The dynamic marks are supplied by the editor, but are in good taste. The four seasons mentioned in the text should be caught in the music by four different moods. July should rhyme with "truly." A moderate tempo would be most suitable.

but in her heart, her   heart, a cold De - cem - - - -
but in her heart, her   heart,   a   cold De - cem - - -
— her   heart,   a   cold   De - cem - -
heart,   but in her heart,   a   cold   De - cem - -

- ber,   but   in   her heart,   but   in   her
- ber, but   in   her   heart,   her   heart,   but   in   her
- ber,   but   in her heart,   but   in _____   her
- ber, _____   but   in her   heart,

heart, her   heart, a cold De - cem - - - - ber.
heart, her   heart,   a   cold De - cem - - - ber.
heart,   a   cold   De - cem - - ber.
but in her heart,   a   cold   De - cem - - ber.

STAN' STILL JORDAN
Fela Sowande

The composer of this Spiritual, a native of Nigeria, was born in 1905. He was educated in England where he taught for a while, and then returned to Lagos, Nigeria, to become the Music Director of the Nigerian Broadcasting Service. He is also an organist as well as a composer. Fela Sowande should be better known in this country, and perhaps this little introduction to his work will arouse an interest in his rather unique approach to the Negro Spiritual. The arrangement is simple; in the opening passage quoted here, there is a slow crescendo, which fades into a slight diminuendo to the refrain which follows. There should be no major conducting problems; however, the vitality of the rhythm should be carefully observed ensuring that, even at a slow tempo, the syncopations are well defined and the difference between ♪. ♪ ♪ and ♪ ♪ ♪ is clear and discernible.

When I get up in Glory, Lord, I can't stan' still.

When I get up in Glory, Lord, I can't stan' still.

When I get up in Glory, Lord, I can't stan' still.

When I get up in Glory, Lord, I can't stan' still.

When I get up in Glory, I can't stan' still.

SAY YE TO THE RIGHTEOUS
From *The Peaceable Kingdom*

Randall Thompson

The final two pages from the first chorus, "Say ye to the righteous" from *The Peaceable Kingdom*, by Randall Thompson. This excerpt calls for a tremendous dynamic range and several different "shapes" of the 4 beat. On the second page the words about "the wicked" should not be legato to contrast with those about "the righteous." The sustained notes in the soprano and alto parts must be very smooth, nevertheless. Begin at the arrow. The tempo marking is Andante con molto, about ♩ = 80.

A SWAN
From *Six Chansons*

Paul Hindemith

Original French poems by Rainer Maria Rilke
English version by Elaine de Sinçay

Another short excerpt, "The Swan," from the *Six Chansons* of Paul Hindemith. The chorale style of the first 4 measures leads to a slightly contrapuntal 3 measures which might be set off by an increase in tempo, which, in turn, settles back to the choralelike quiet of the beginning. Notice the climax of the line at "A loved one" which is emphasized here by a double piano, rather than a forte. This must be practiced, for it is a stunning effect when properly executed.

QUAND IL SURVIENT
Pierre de la Rue

The Secular Chanson, "Quand il survient," was written by Pierre de la Rue, a contemporary and compatriot of Josquin des Préz. There are great similarities between the styles of the two men. (The works of Pierre de la Rue are enjoying a general renaissance.) The text consists of advice given to a combatant, concerning his attitude toward his adversary. Start about mf, allowing the line to make the natural crescendi and diminuendi. Do not allow the men to overshadow the upper parts; the range of the soprano and alto is quite low. In old notation of this kind, some notes are held across the bar lines; however, they are not repeated. A space is left in this manner:

Old notation   New notation

is performed:

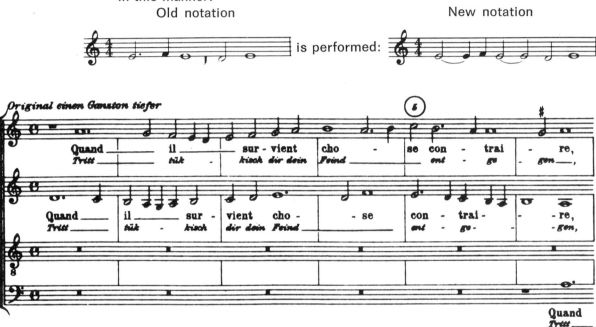

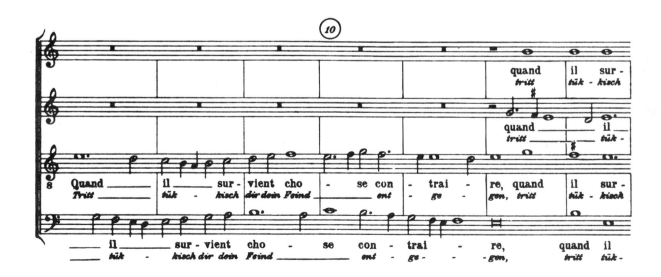

132

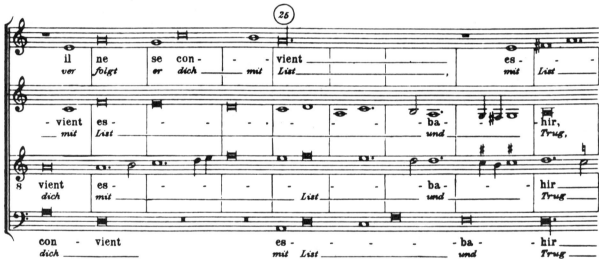

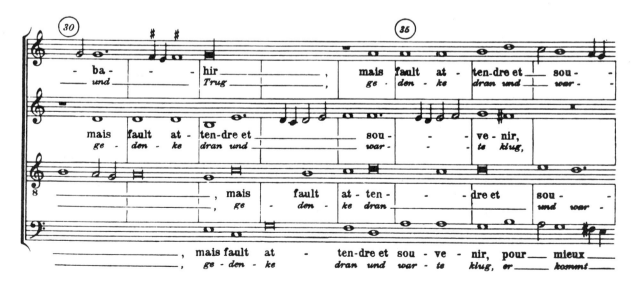

PROPTER MAGNAM GLORIAM
From *Gloria*

Antonio Vivaldi

Edited by Mason Martens

"Propter Magnam Gloriam" comprises the fifth movement of Vivaldi's *Gloria* for soli, mixed chorus, and orchestra. The breve sign at the opening indicates that the half note gets one beat. When performing this piece it is particularly important to keep the spirit buoyant and the rhythm energetic. Do not retard in measures 10 and 11 and do go on for two bars or so into the stretto portion of the fugue seeing that the excitement keeps going through the longer note values and the noncontrapuntal style of the cadence; the spirit *must not* need to be rekindled at the beginning of the stretto (measure 12). ($\quad$ = 92)

3 ROUNDS IN $\frac{4}{4}$ TIME

The round by Samuel Webbe, whose life and work were discussed under "3 Rounds in $\frac{3}{4}$ Time," is quite simple and straightforward, while the other two take a bit of rehearsing to perform well. John Callcott (1766–1821) was a prolific composer of secular music. In his canon he makes references to two of the famous books on the history of music of the eighteenth century, one by Dr. Charles Burney, the other by Sir Johns Hawkins. The inference in the text makes clear which of the two scholars the composer venerates. In this round one is instructed to leave out the passage in brackets until the third voice has entered; in other words, the first two renditions of the tune go up to the first beat of the fourth full measure and then skip to the second beat (quarter rest) of the ninth full measure. Do not observe the *fermata* until the last time the piece is performed. Stephen Paxton (1735–1787) was another composer of secular music and a well-known cellist of his time. His canon is obviously a spoof and should be performed to bring out the humor, irony, satire, or pathos of the words. Be careful not to observe the *Vivace* marking too literally, for the sixteenth notes have words to be sung and these should come out clearly.

The Historians

J.W. Callcott

Holy Matrimony

Stephen Paxton

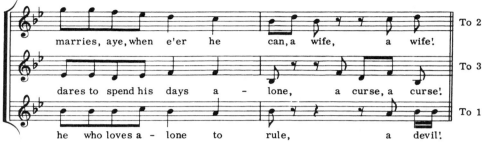

marries, aye, when e'er he   can, a   wife,   a   wife!   To 2

dares to spend his   days   a - lone,   a curse, a   curse!   To 3

he   who loves a - lone   to   rule,   a   devil!   To 1

Celia's Charms

Samuel Webbe

Andante [con moto]

1 Would   you   know   my   Ce - lia's   charms,

2 I'm sure she's for-ti -tude,   I'm sure she's for-ti -tude and

3 She's on - ly   thir-ty,

4 Ce - lia ought to   strive,   For cer - tain -

Would   you   know   my   Ce - lia's   charms,   Which

truth,   for - ti - tude   and   truth,   for - ti - tude   and

she's on - ly   thir - ty,   she's on - ly   thir - ty   lo - vers

-ly   she's fif - ty - five,   she's fif - ty -

now ____ ex - cite ____ my   fierce a - larms?   To 2

truth, To gain the heart of   ev - ery   youth, of   ev-ery   youth.   To 3

now, The rest are gone, I   can't tell   how;   No   long - er   To 4

-five,   cer - tain-ly she's   fif - ty - five.   To 1

KYRIE ELEISON

From *Mass for Four Voices*

William Byrd

Edited by Edmund H. Fellowes

William Byrd (1543–1623) was certainly one of the most prolific and influential of all early British composers. He wrote secular as well as sacred music. The *Mass for Four Voices* is an example of great contrapuntal skill used with the greatest of taste. Analyze the piece thoroughly so that the repeated motifs come out very clearly.

Original pitch a tone higher

Chris - te___ e - lei - son,   Chris - te e - lei - son,

Chris - te e - lei - - son,   Chris - te e -

Chris - te e - lei - son,   Chris - te e - lei - - son, Chris -

Chris - te e - lei - son,   Chris - te e - lei -

Chris - te e - lei - son,   Chris - te e - lei - son.

-lei - - son,   Chris - te e - lei - son.

- te e - lei - son,   Chris - te e - lei - - son.

- - son,   Chris - te e - lei - - - son.

HE THAT SHALL ENDURE TO THE END

From *Elijah*

Felix Mendelssohn

"He That Shall Endure" from Mendelssohn's *Elijah* resembles a chorale. The student conductor should not find this piece particularly difficult. However, it is necessary to observe all dynamics; the entrances should be smooth, and the contrapuntal sections, which appear after the first page, should bring out the important melodic elements.

LET EV'RY HEART BE MERRY
Horatio Vecchi

"Let Ev'ry Heart Be Merry" is a happy little madrigal by the Italian composer Horatio Vecchi (1550–1605). The unit of measure is the half note; it is suggested that the first and second beat of the first measure be given to ensure a secure attack. The dynamics were added by an editor and seem in order. However, if it is felt that others may be more effective they should be tried and compared. For instance, each set of "fa-la-las" might be sung with a variation of dynamics.

ACHIEVED IS THE GLORIOUS WORK
From *The Creation*

Franz Joseph Haydn

This is a chorus from Haydn's masterpiece *The Creation.* The mood throughout is one of rejoicing. The bouncing eighth notes should give character to the beat, and underlie all longer notes in order to retain rhythmic vitality. Make sure that the off-beat entrances are absolutely together and do not interfere with the accompaniment of cutoffs.

LO COUNTRY SPORTS
Thomas Weelkes

Here is a lovely madrigal by the British composer Thomas Weelkes (1575–1623) written around 1597. It is a lively piece, but the tempo must be determined by how fast and clearly the chorus is able to negotiate the eighth notes. The beauty of this edition is that it does not clutter the page with expression or tempo markings. It is therefore up to the conductor to determine the most effective rendition of the piece, considering the spirit of the text and some of the performance practices of the times. The sixteenth-century pieces contained in this anthology should prompt discussions regarding performance practices applicable to each of them. The ranges of the voices also is a factor in the successful presentation of this madrigal. The soprano and tenor parts are quite low, and balance will be problematical throughout. One answer to this dilemma could be redistribution of forces. Mix half the altos into the soprano section and put half of the sopranos into the alto section; then do the same thing with the men. The altos and basses can be extremely helpful in strengthening the rather low *tessitura* all the way through.

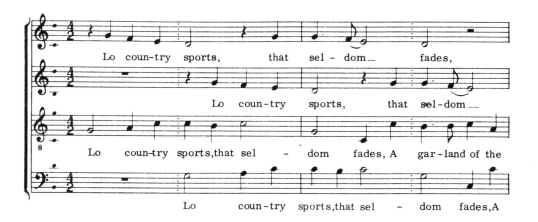

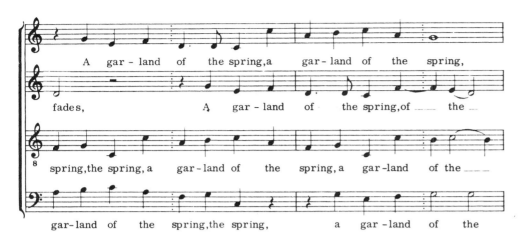

A gar - land of the spring, a gar - land of the spring,

fades,   A gar - land of the spring, of ___ the ___

spring, the spring, a gar - land of the spring, a gar - land of the ___

gar - land of the spring, the spring,   a gar - land of the

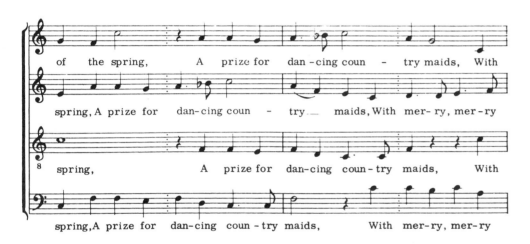

of the spring,   A prize for dan - cing coun - try maids, With

spring, A prize for dan - cing coun - try ___ maids, With mer- ry, mer - ry

spring,   A prize for dan - cing coun - try maids,   With

spring, A prize for dan - cing coun - try maids,   With mer- ry, mer - ry

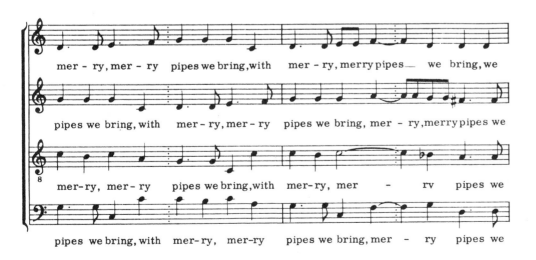

mer - ry, mer - ry pipes we bring, with mer - ry, merry pipes ___ we bring, we

pipes we bring, with mer - ry, mer - ry pipes we bring, mer - ry, merry pipes we

mer - ry, mer - ry pipes we bring, with mer - ry, mer - ry pipes we

pipes we bring, with mer - ry, mer - ry pipes we bring, mer - ry pipes we

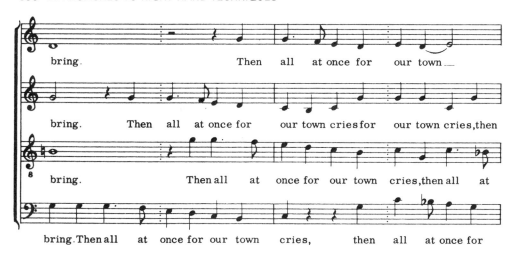

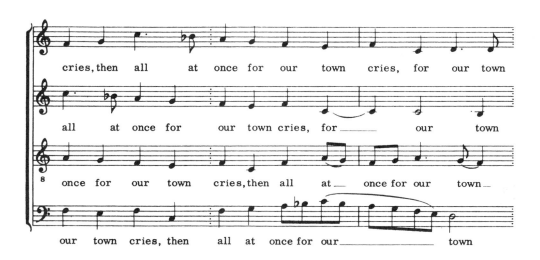

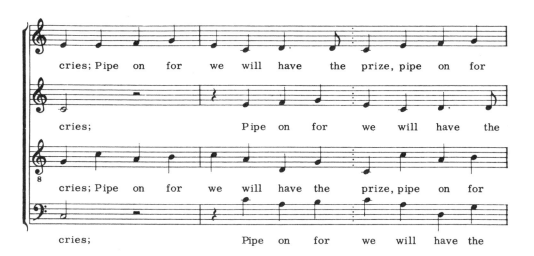

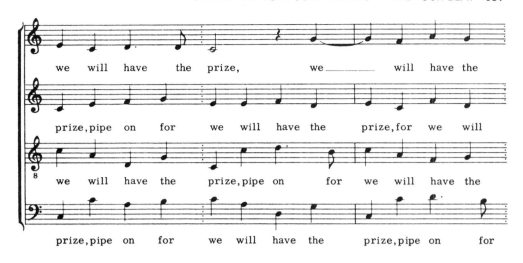

we will have the prize,   we_____ will have the
prize,pipe on for   we will have the   prize,for we will
we will have the   prize,pipe on   for   we will have the
prize,pipe on for   we will have the   prize,pipe on   for

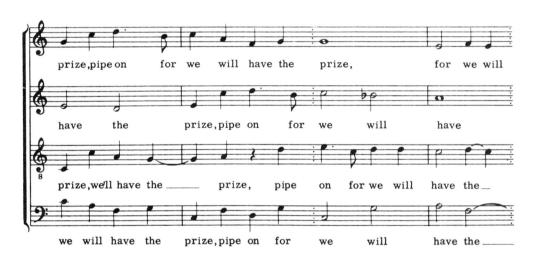

prize,pipe on   for   we will have the   prize,   for we will
have   the   prize,pipe on   for   we   will   have
prize,we'll have the ____   prize,   pipe   on   for we will   have the __
we will have the   prize,pipe on   for   we   will   have the _____

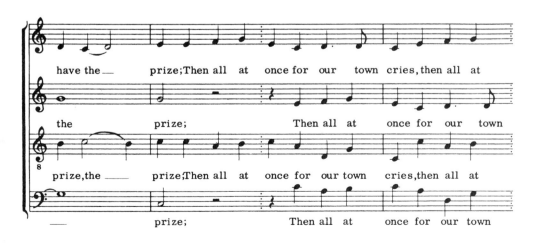

have the __   prize;Then all at   once for our   town cries,then all at
the   prize;   Then all at   once for our   town
prize,the ____   prize;Then all at   once for our town   cries,then all at
____   prize;   Then all   at   once for our town

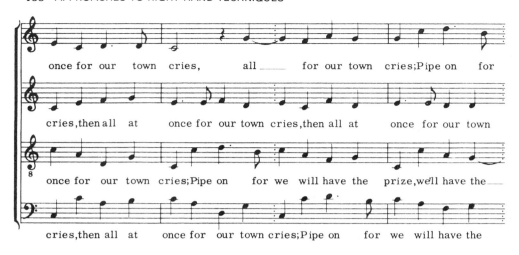

A JUBILANT SONG
Music by Norman Dello Joio

Words adapted from Walt Whitman

This short excerpt from *A Jubilant Song* by Norman Dello Joio gives the student conductor a chance to practice rhythmic dichotomy. While one part of the chorus is "bouncing" along, the others are singing sustained lines. Only the "inner beat" of the bouncing line should influence the sustained portion. The smooth flow must not be disrupted. Later on in our analysis of choral conducting we will show how the left hand is extensively used to define a separate rhythm. Allegro ♩ = 116.

INSCRIPTION

From *Symphony for Voices*

Music by Roy Harris

Words by Walt Whitman

Measures 39 through 61 of the third movement of Roy Harris' *Symphony for Voices* are difficult to conduct because the countersubject of the fugue has a different rhythmic and emotional character from the primary, smooth subject. The joyous nature of both should be the unifying element; however, the "lift" of the countersubject must be revealed by the conductor. $\frac{4}{4}$, M.M. *ca.* $\quad$ = 126. It is suggested that the two subjects be sung separately at first to establish their characteristics clearly before they are put together.

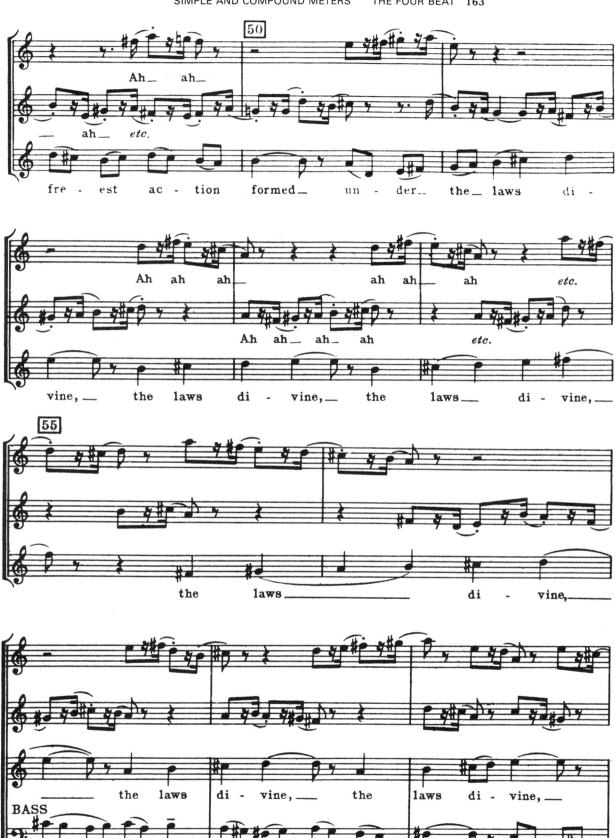

LARK

Music by Aaron Copland Words by Genevieve Taggard

This is a very short quotation from a wonderful choral piece by Aaron Copland. The work has many intricate passages especially preceding and following this spot. These six measures were chosen for the student to practice over and over again. The pattern is 2 + 3, 3 + 2, 2 + 3, 3 + 2, 2 + 3, 3 + 2, conducted in two strokes. Repeat this excerpt several times at a good speed. The marking is Allegro ♩ = 138. This is the kind of exercise each student in the class should try and master.

AN EGG
From *Homer's Woe*

Jack Beeson

Jack Beeson wrote twelve rounds for treble voices under the title *Homer's Woe.* (The author of the text is anonymous.) No. 10 in the set is called "The Egg." It is a three-part canon, and each voice should sing its part twice all the way through, in order to solve this musical riddle. Be sure you follow it in your mind and signal the second entrance for each of the three parts. The upbeat of the beginning will of course be the fifth beat of the measure in which the voice will enter to repeat the canon. The dynamics may be varied by having the first statement sung forte and the second piano, or vice-versa.

In mar-ble halls as white as milk, Lined with a skin as soft_ as silk, With-

in a foun-tain crys-tal-clear, A gold - en ap-ple doth ap - pear,_ A gold - en ap-ple doth ap-

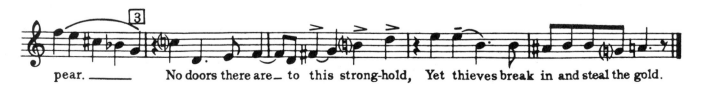

pear. _____ No doors there are_ to this strong-hold, Yet thieves break in and steal the gold.

WAINAMOINEN MAKES MUSIC
Music by Zoltán Kodály

Text taken from "Kalevala, the land of heroes."

Translated by W. F. Kirby

Many folk songs have two traits in common: (1) they have a limited range, and (2) they often have a strange meter or additive rhythm. These characteristics apply to folk music all over the world. "Wainamionen Makes Music" by Zoltán Kodály is based on folk legend. The pattern of the 5 beats is generally 2 + 3; some measures, however, (especially 8, 10, 11 and 13) are 3 + 2. The tempo should be about ♩ = 92.

PSALM
From "Psalm and Prayer of David"

Walter Piston

Psalm and Prayer of David is the second of only two works for chorus written by Walter Piston. It is for mixed chorus and seven instruments. The pattern includes two unequal strokes, but it is evident from the music when the conductor should divide the measure into 3 + 2 or 2 + 3. Only the first measure is doubtful in its construction; however it seems advisable to use a 3 + 2 pattern since the second and fourth measures, containing similar music, are divided in this fashion.

I WILL LIFT UP MINE EYES

Psalm 121

Paul Ben-Haim

A short excerpt from the setting of the Psalm 121 by the dean of Israeli composers, Paul Ben-Haim. It may be performed in either English or Hebrew. The tempo should be moderate and project a sustained feeling. A suggested marking would be ♩ = 88.

SING JOYFULLY
Music by Herman Berlinski
Words from Psalm 81

In this broad and joyful opening of Herman Berlinski's setting of Psalm 81, the conductor should set a tempo determined by the sixteenth notes. These must not feel rushed, yet the spirit of exuberance should be sustained: ♩ = 84 would be a good tempo. The trumpet part is not necessary for the practice of the piece in class, but it is most effective when used during a religious service.

PSALM OF BROTHERHOOD
Music by Heinrich Schalit

Words from Psalm 133

Here we have the first few pages of Heinrich Schalit's setting of words from Psalm 133. It may be sung in either English or Hebrew. The beat is straightforward, but be sure it moves along (suggested ♩ = 80) and that the phrase ending is not retarded, except where it is marked on the top of the fourth page. Also watch the dynamics at the alto entrance. Because of the low range of the alto, hold down the strength of the tenors and basses. Also watch the soprano entrance for the same reason.

174

SIXTH MADRIGAL
From *The Unicorn*

Gian Carlo Menotti

An excerpt from the Sixth Madrigal of the "Madrigal Fable" called *The Unicorn, the Gorgon and the Manticore* by Gian Carlo Menotti. The tempo is rather slow, $\flat = 72$, and the feeling should be that of a sixteenth-century madrigal with crisp rhythms and smoothly flowing lines. The sudden stop occurs because the meter changes several times. It is important to practice the 6 beat in this excerpt without regard for further complexities.

Cov - er my head, ___ si - lence the night - in - gale.

head with a black veil.

Cov - er my head ___ with a black veil. Muf - fle the horn and the

Cov - er my head. Muf - fle the horn and the

Muf - fle the horn and the lute, si - lence the night - in - gale, ___

Muf - fle the horn and the lute, si - lence the night - in - gale, ___

lute, ___ si - lence the ___

lute, si - lence the night - in - gale, ___ the night - in - gale, ___

YOU HAVE RAVISHED MY HEART
Stephen Chatman

Text from the Song of Solomon 4:9-16*

A short excerpt from an anthem on a beautiful but rather neglected text from the "Song of Solomon," this piece is by a talented American composer now living in Canada and teaching at the University of British Columbia in Vancouver. It begins very softly and slowly makes a crescendo from measure 9 to the climax of this section in measure 16. From this high point on, it slowly settles down to a soft cadence in e minor. This is not the end of the piece, but only the first third of it. Notice that contrary to much "common practice" the tempo slows between measures 11 and 12 right in the center of the crescendo, increasing the intensity of the climax even more. The time for the diminuendo from *forte* to *piano* is much shorter than the preceding crescendo; therefore, the diminuendo should be begun immediately after the fourth beat of measure 16. The composer has zealously marked the phrases, so it is necessary for the conductor to follow these suggestions meticulously and see that the breaths are taken to coincide with the endings of the long slurs.

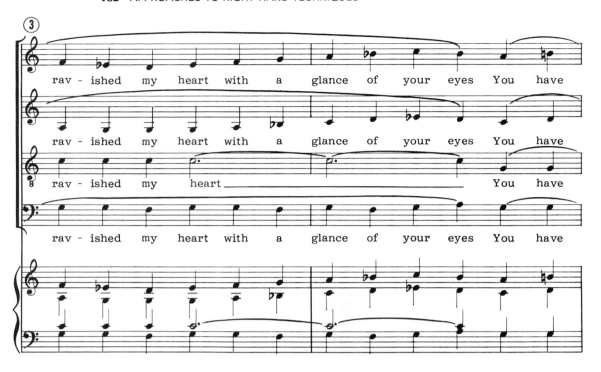

CHORALE
Music by David Diamond
Words by James Agee

This is the beginning of a long choral piece written by David Diamond in 1950. Actually the excerpt should have appeared in Chapter 2, but it is purposely placed here to give the student practice in fitting equal eighth notes into three closely related patterns. There is an accent change between $\frac{6}{8}$, $\frac{9}{8}$ and $\frac{3}{4}$. The exercise of the differing eighth-note patterns using this beautifully sustained piece should be most beneficial as an introduction to the next chapter: $\frac{6}{8}$ should be conducted in a 6 pattern, even the duplet measures, while $\frac{9}{8}$ is a divided 3 and also $\frac{3}{4}$ is a divided 3 pattern. The ending in measure 13 is abrupt, for a new section starts after a quarter general pause.

Poem from PERMIT ME VOYAGE, Yale University Press

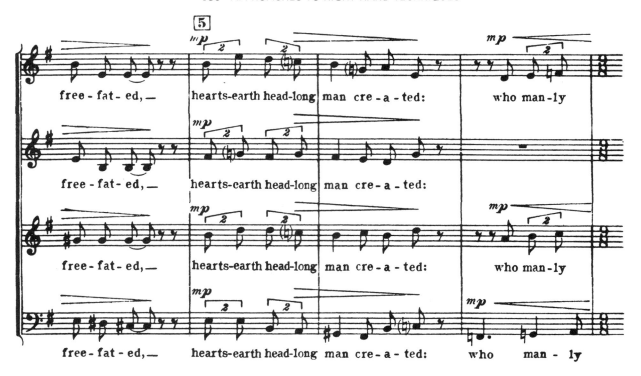

THE CHERUBIC HYMN
Howard Hanson

Text from the Greek Catholic Liturgy of Saint John Chrysostom
Arranged for use in English by Stephen A. Hurlbut.

The 7 beat in this short excerpt from the very popular *Cherubic Hymn* by Howard Hanson should not be difficult since the same pattern is kept throughout. As in the 5 beat, be very sure that the "one" and the "five" strokes are not exactly the same, even though they are both down beats. It is suggested that the 1 beat be a bit larger in all instances. Piu animato ♩ = 66.

DIES IRAE
From *War Requiem*

Benjamin Britten

Usually one cannot find many sustained passages in $\frac{7}{4}$ without some change of meter; however, this excerpt from the *War Requiem* by Benjamin Britten is certainly an exception. As a matter of fact, the "Dies Irae" is followed by another $\frac{7}{4}$ in slow motion——the beautiful setting for solo and chorus of the "Lacrimosa." The "Dies Irae" is a fast and furious passage; the quarter note equals 160, but the pattern remains 4 + 3 or 2 + 2 + 3. Even though the last Allegro marking is ♩ = 132 (at 45) it is related to the beginning of the "Dies Irae" which is marked ♩ = 160.

FINALE From *Kaddish, Symphony No. 3*
Music by Leonard Bernstein

Vocal score by
Abraham Kaplan - Ruth Mense.

This is an extremely difficult and exciting passage from Leonard Bernstein's Third Symphony. Here we have a $\frac{7}{8}$ pattern in 3 which is always divided 2 + 2 + 3. The grace note should almost be on the beat so that nothing is "robbed" from the rhythm. Sh' is pronounced like the French "Le," and the translation of the words is "May His great Name be blessed in all eternity." In performing the excerpt during class, two soloists should be designated to execute the children's chorus parts and in preparation of the performance all should clap their respective rhythms, then sing the notes on the syllable "do" and finally perform, watching the accents as well as the dynamics carefully. (Begin at A) Tempo ♩ = 138.

UNTIL DAY AND NIGHT SHALL CEASE
From *Hebrew Cantata*

Music by Harold Shapero
Words by Jehuda Halevi

The 8 and 9 beats are always subdivided into a 3 and 4 pattern; it might be beneficial, however, to do an actual excerpt in $\frac{8}{4}$ time. One large 4 pattern, subdivided as it is here, should make all subdivisions in the 4 pattern (such as a divided $\frac{4}{4}$ or a compound divided $\frac{12}{8}$) an easy matter. This is the eighth and final movement from Harold Shapero's *Hebrew Cantata*; the texts are taken from the poet Jehuda Halevi, who lived in Spain from 1086–1140.

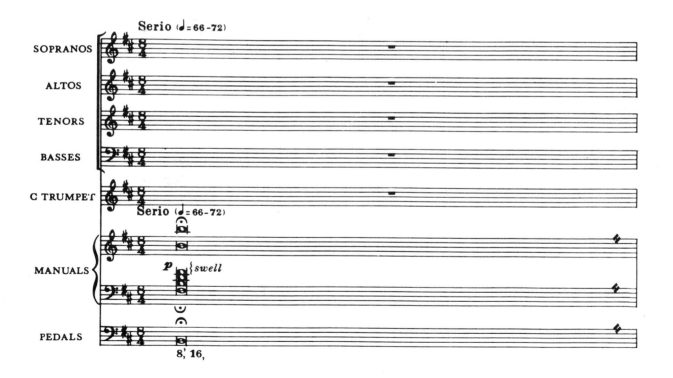

CHICHESTER PSALMS
No. 3

Leonard Bernstein

Leonard Bernstein's *Chichester Psalms* has a rather unusual rhythm that must be sustained during most of the third and last movement. The tempo marking is "Peacefully flowing," $\quad$ = 120. In order to make this sound like a real $\frac{10}{4}$, rather than two $\frac{5}{4}$'s, Bernstein gives the following directions. "This should be conducted in the shape of a divided 4 beat, adding an extra inner beat on *2* and *4* (1 + 2 + + 3 + 4 + +)." The words from the Psalm 131 mean: "Surely I have calmed myself, as a child that is weaned of his mother."

2
Changing
Meter Signature
With a
Constant Pulse Symbol

Many works in twentieth century music do not sustain one uniform meter throughout their entire duration. Quite a few pieces change meters frequently, others dwell a bit longer in one time signature before switching to another. Pre-Renaissance and other music of the more distant past, governed by word accents and dance forms and composed without bar lines, tend to have a greater occurrence of meter change than the music of the Baroque, Classical, and Romantic Periods.

For pragmatic purposes the changes of meter have been divided into two separate chapters. Chapter 2 will deal with changes of beats while the common denominator of a quarter, half, or eighth note remains constant. Chapter 3 will discuss interchangeable denominators.

The first important fact to remember is that even though the number of beats in a measure may vary, the tempo remains constant, unless otherwise indicated. $\frac{4}{4} - \frac{5}{4} - \frac{6}{4}$ does not mean that the 5 or 6 quarter notes must occupy the same time span as the 4 quarters in the first measure of the sequence, but rather that these are longer by one or two counts.

Two examples in this chapter pose slightly different problems and have been included here to point up important tempo changes. The Bach example and the Janequin Chanson deal with tempo problems in addition to changing meters. The latter should introduce to the student the fifteenth-through early sixteenth-century problems of proportional notation; further examples might be sought out.

Great clarity and assurance must adorn the first beat of every measure. This is especially crucial when dividing a $\frac{5}{4}$ into 2 + 3 or 3 + 2, or a $\frac{7}{4}$ into 3 + 4, 4 + 3, 3 + 2 + 2, 2 + 2 + 3 or 2 + 3 + 2. If a complex compound rhythm is not divided by the composer or editor with the use of dotted lines, barring eighth notes or some other similar designation, the conductor should decide on his conducting pattern with help of the word accents.

If the beat patterns practiced in the previous chapter are now "second nature," the following exercises should not be too overwhelming. It should be stressed again that the more inner-beat feeling the gestures have, the more vibrant and exciting will be the rhythmic performance. Try for this reason to gauge the tempo and the rhythm by the fastest notes present in each piece, or if there are no fast notes, superimpose an "inner feeling" of fast-moving units upon each beat.

GOD'S TIME IS THE BEST
From *Cantata No. 106*

J. S. Bach

Edited by Frank Damrosch

Most examples in Chapter 2 deal with the problem of changing meters from measure to measure without necessarily affecting the mood or tempo of the piece. The chapter commences, however, with a quite different problem, namely, sectional changes of beat patterns which also initiate completely new emotional and psychological feelings of the different portions of the work. In other words, this powerful excerpt from Bach's Cantata No. 106 tests the student's ability to change beat patterns smoothly, while the tempo, the mood, and the dynamics of the piece change with the meter. It is important for the student to "feel" that the last measure of the first page is a preparation for the middle part of the piece; the two chords which lead into the adagio assai are prepared for several measures ahead by a gradual ritardando. The editor has suggested a ♪ = 72 metronome marking; but a ♩ = 44 marking (♪ = 88) would sound more vital. (The two chords should also be tried at ♩ = 44). Both speeds should be tested. After the first two beats it would be best not to subdivide.

BLESS YE THE LORD
Music by M. Ippolitof-Ivanof

Arranged by Peter J. Wilhousky

Words adapted from Psalm 103 by John Moment

This is a portion of the Russian Orthodox Liturgy, set to music by Ippolitof-Ivanof. There are editions of this little piece which do not change the meter; the one by Wilhousky, presented here, does change it in order to stress the chantlike nature of the piece, give it a freer flow, and by means of notes instead of words write out an implicit ritard. Tenuto marks should be placed on the first two notes; then make the half note equal 108, followed by a retard to Tempo I, which would be about ♩ = 96.

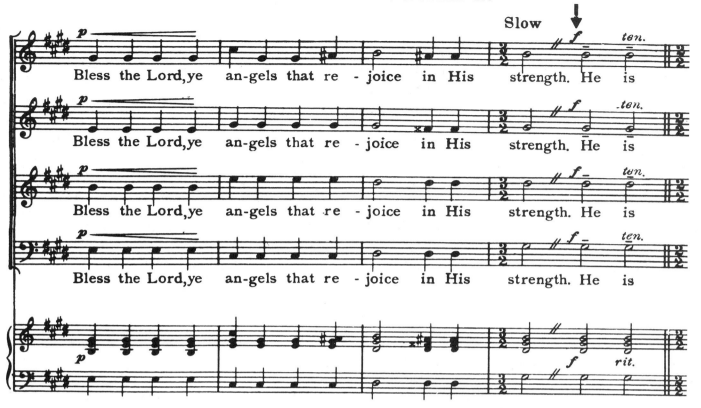

Bless the Lord, ye an-gels that re - joice in His strength. He is

gra - cious, kind and full of com - pas - sion, ev - er just, But He

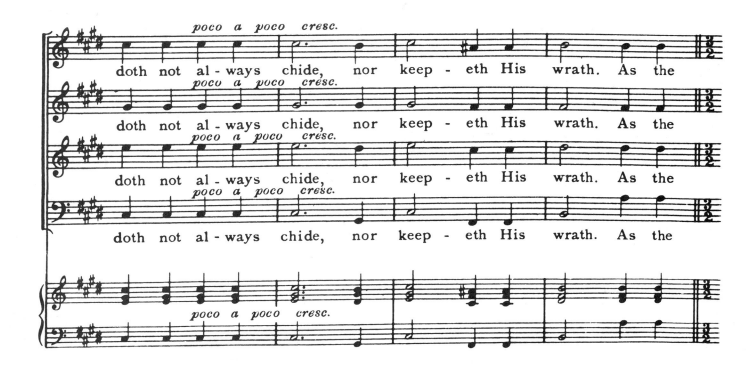

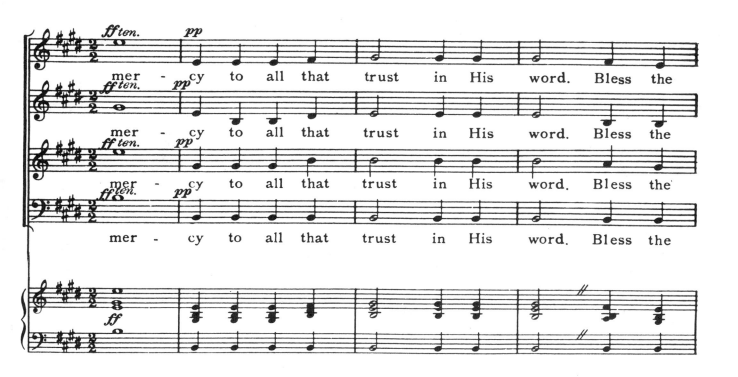

Tempo I

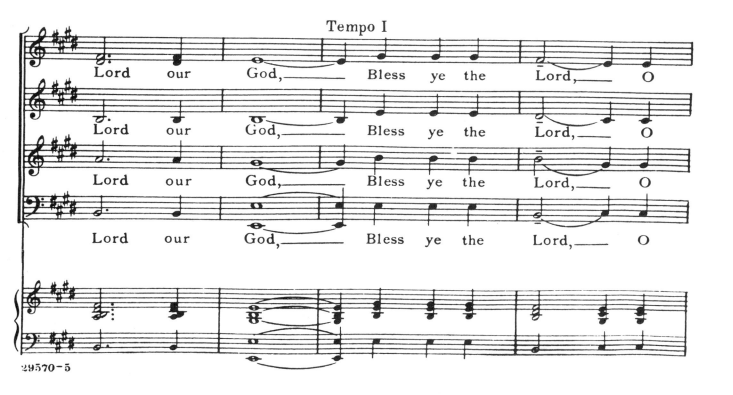

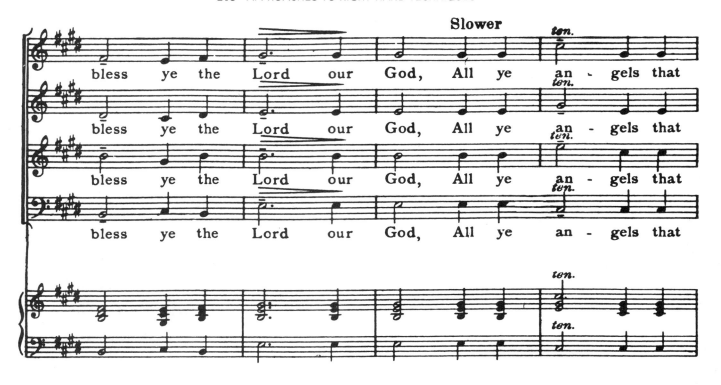

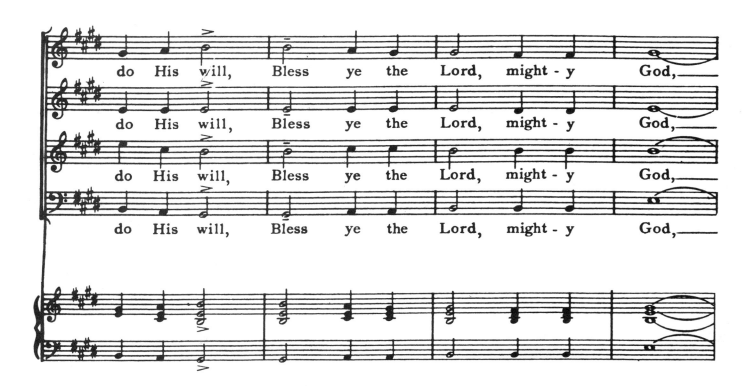

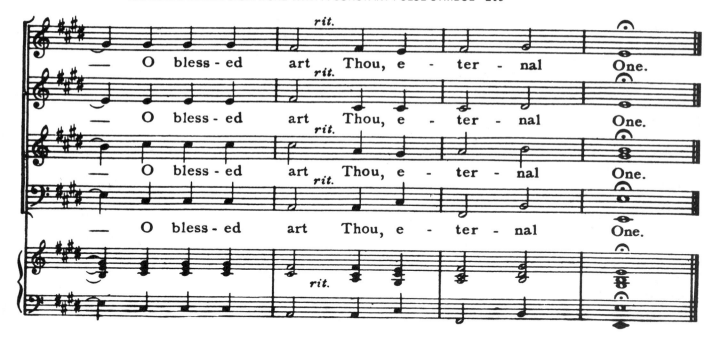

TRESVES DAMOURS
No. 2 From *Ten Chansons*

Clement Janequin   Edited by Albert Seay

Sixteenth-century music often alternates, for short periods, between duple and triple meters. The lovely chanson, "Tresves Damours," by Clement Janequin contains a sudden triple meter passage which makes the half-note unit suddenly faster, for a measure of $\frac{3}{2}$ equals the previous measure of $\frac{2}{2}$ and vice versa when reversed. Practice this change until it sounds very natural. The words of the chanson deal with the falseness of love when it is founded on pretence, and the conviction that real love comes from the heart.

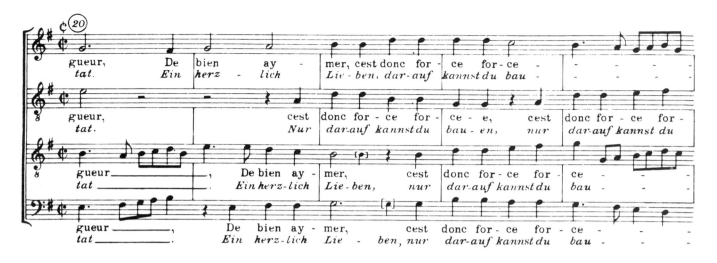

MAGNIFICAT
Thomas Tomkins

From *Second Service*

Edited by Ivor Atkins

Revised by Watkins Shaw

Thomas Tomkins who wrote in the sixteenth and early seventeenth centuries did not specify the changes in meter; bar lines have been provided by the editor, however, for contemporary use. Maintain a steady half note equal to about 84 throughout the piece and be careful not to overemphasize the downbeats on the bar lines which have been supplied.

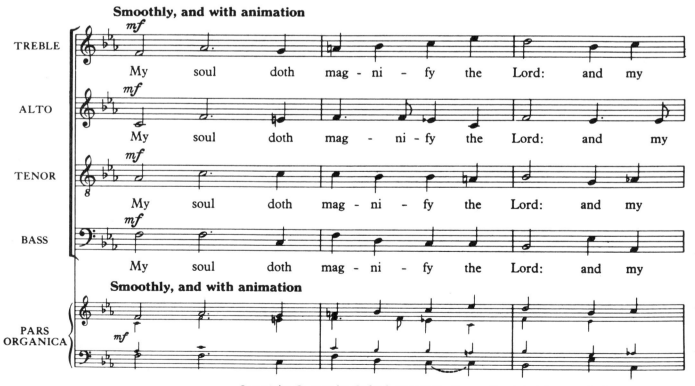

GLORY TO GOD
Alan Hovhaness

This passage from the cantata "Glory to God" by Alan Hovhaness resembles a chorale and maintains a constant half note throughout. The tempo is allegro with the half note at 120. It is written with an accompaniment of brass, percussion and organ, but it should be sung a capella, occasionally, during rehearsals, to test the accuracy of the pitch. The object of this passage is to build slowly, from a very quiet beginning to a fortissimo, which is maintained to the end.

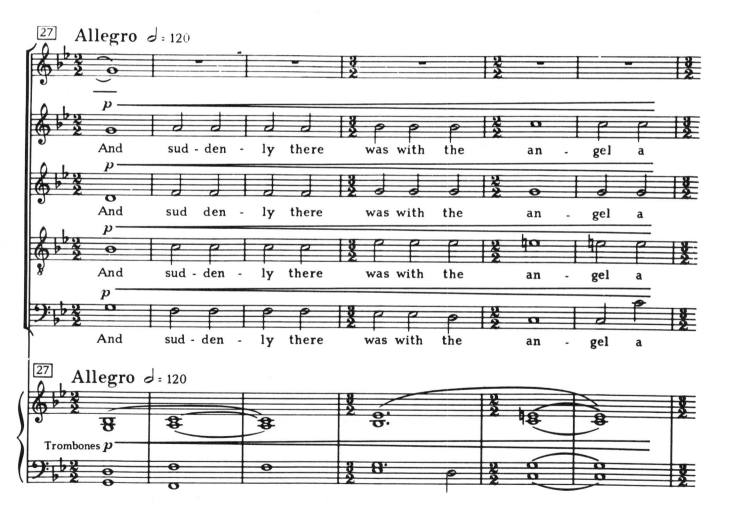

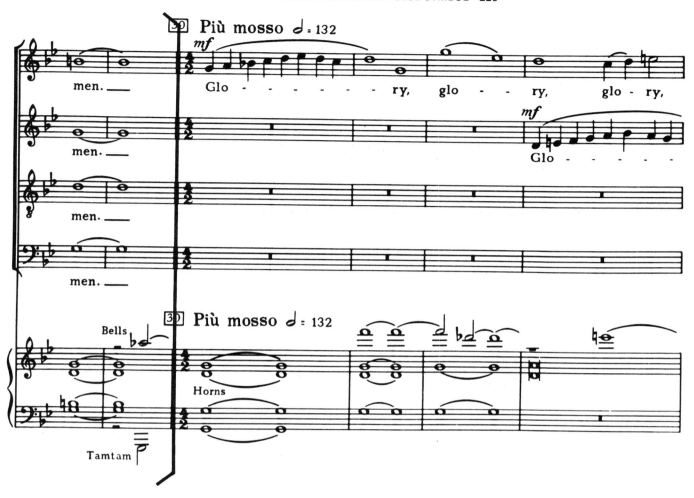

PSALM 51

From *Pilgrim Psalms*

Ross Lee Finney

According to Ross Lee Finney, the music of his collection *Pilgrim Psalms* was sung in America for a hundred years after it was brought here by the Pilgrims. The roots can be traced to a book published in Amsterdam in 1612 by Henry Ainsworth. Finney has tried to stay as close to the original tunes as possible. He provided, here, a beautiful setting of Psalm 51. The old spellings, and the awkardness of matching poetic and musical accents may present some problems at first, but they become increasingly harmonious with familiarity, and cannot be changed without altering the primitive quality of these lovely pieces. The many holds should not be overly stressed, but used, rather, as breathing places. Start at the arrow; Largo = 40.

FOG

From *Five Scenes*

Music by David Epstein

* Words by Carl Sandburg

"Fog" from David Epstein's *Five Scenes*, based on Carl Sandberg's *Chicago Poems*. In order to achieve the degree of articulation desired by the composer, it would be advisable to subdivide the beats of measures that have eighth notes marked with dashes; for example, beats 3 + 4 of measure 1, beats 1 + 2 of measure 5, and possibly beat 3 of measure 3. The latter could be tried both ways. Under no circumstances should the whole piece be subdivided.

I NEVER SAW A MOOR
Music by Robert Muczynski
Words by Emily Dickinson

The short choral piece, "I never saw a Moor," by Robert Muczynski provides a very simple exercise in changing meters, with the quarter note remaining constant. The $\frac{5}{4}$ pattern is always 2 + 3, so no problems should arise. The style is not difficult to grasp aurally, but it would save time to use the piano when the piece is first attempted.

VIRTUE
Music by Nicolas Flagello

Words by George Herbert

"Virtue," by Nicolas Flagello, provides the chance to practice entrance signals and maintain visual contact, while varying the beat patterns and keeping the quarter note constant. After the fermata at the end of measure 8 the conductor has two approaches at his disposal. First use the cutoff of measure 8 to signal the downbeat of the next, and second, cutoff, completely followed by a silence, before continuing with the first beat of the next measure.

THE 23rd PSALM
Herbert Fromm

The setting of Psalm 23 by Herbert Fromm mixes two pastoral colors: the flute sound of the accompaniment and the chantlike melody of the choral portion. There is no set pattern of $\frac{2}{4}$ $\frac{3}{4}$ in this excerpt, so it is important to establish it ahead of time. The phrase endings, especially at "in green pastures," should be clearly defined. The charm of the piece is emphasized by following the number of beats strictly, without retardations, with the possible exception of the triplet on the words "paths for His." A choir tempo is suggested: (Tempo ritmico) ♪ = 56.

*) NOTE: The flute passages in the introduction, in the two interludes and in the last 3 measures are to be played by the organ, if no flute is available.

DOMINE FILI
From *Gloria*

Francis Poulenc

Francis Poulenc's "Gloria" was written in 1959, and since its first performance by the Boston Symphony Orchestra, it has become part of the standard repertoire. This excerpt from the fourth movement ($\frac{4}{4}$) is a very joyful piece. It has a metronome marking of $\quartdot$ = 112. Crispness and a bouncing rhythm characterize the eighth notes; the accompanying sixteenths move rapidly and smoothly; the quarters are sustained to their full value.

IN CERTAINTY OF SONG
No. 3

Music by Wallingford Riegger
Words by Catherine Harris

This is an excerpt from the third movement of Wallingford Riegger's Cantata, *In Certainty of Song*, with words by Catherine Harris. This should present no conductorial problems but be sure that the change of tempo at the Allegro (♩ = *ca.* 112) comes off smoothly. It is suggested that the cutoff in measure 5 be used as the downbeat to Ⓐ, and then that it be tried with a complete stop after measure 5.

LAMENT
From *The Hour-Glass*

Music by Irving Fine

Words by Ben Jonson

A few measures from the fifth movement of a six-movement, a cappella choral cycle called *The Hour-Glass* by Irving Fine based on a text by Ben Jonson. The eighth notes should flow freely. Subdividing the beat should be avoided because it would cause the rhythm to drag. The soprano must have a sustained quality while the others "punctuate," and each phrase should flow naturally into the next without sounding sectional.

AWAKE! DO NOT CAST US OFF
Music by Samuel Adler

Words from Psalm 44 and an ancient Hebrew poem

Measures 32 through 51 of my anthem to words of Psalm 44, is an exercise in alternating one- and two-beat patterns. I would suggest all $\frac{3}{4}$ and $\frac{2}{4}$ measures be conducted in one, while all $\frac{4}{4}$ and $\frac{5}{4}$ bars be conducted in two. The bars are divided in the manner in which they are printed. Feel and use strong accentuations for these chantlike phrases on the first beats of the measures. Allegro molto $\quad \lozenge = 76$.

GREENER PASTURES
Music by Jack Beeson
Words Anonymous

"Greener Pastures" is another round by Jack Beeson; this time it is fully written out. The composer has provided a note to the conductor at the bottom of the first page. When conducting the 5 + 5 or the 4 + 5 divisions, the first beat of each measure should differ from the fifths or sixths, respectively.

Oh that I were where I would be, Then ___ would I be where I am not; But where I am ___ there ___ I must be, ___ And ___

Oh that I were where I would be, Then ___ would I be where I am

* For the convenience of conductor and singers the over-all structure is shown by barlines, which designate a regular alternation between a unit of 10 beats and a unit of 9. These units are usually subdivided, respectively, into 2 units of 5 and a unit of 4 followed by a unit of 5. Rhythmic-verbal accentuation, when it does not conform to this subdivision, is indicated by auxiliary vertical strokes, also intended to carry strong barline accents.

GLORIA
From *Mass*

Igor Stravinsky

Igor Stravinsky has probably been more responsible for the widening of our rhythmic horizon than any other twentieth-century composer. Here is a short excerpt from his Mass for Mixed Chorus and Double Wind Quintet. The metronome marking is ♩ = 72; therefore, the ♪ note equals 144. Conduct these two pages in two different ways. First, try a 3, 2 and 4 beat pattern for the $\frac{3}{8}$, $\frac{2}{8}$ and $\frac{4}{8}$. Then try using a 1 beat for the $\frac{3}{8}$ and the $\frac{2}{8}$ and a 2 beat gesture for the $\frac{4}{8}$.

THE DEATH OF THE BISHOP OF BRINDISI
Gian Carlo Menotti

A short excerpt from Gian Carlo Menotti's dramatic cantata *The Death of the Bishop of Brindisi*. This work was written in 1962–1963 for bass and soprano solo, children's chorus, mixed chorus and orchestra. This is a very fast and powerful passage to be sung, almost entirely, either in unison or in two parts. The $\frac{12}{8}$ is, of course, in a 4-beat pattern, the $\frac{9}{8}$ in 3, and the $\frac{6}{8}$ in a 2 beat.

* The scoring of this work does not always permit a reduction for piano two hands. In this and other passages it is suggested that either brace may be used by the pianist.

KYRIE
From *Missa de Angelis*

Robert Crane

Here is the "Kyrie" from the *Missa de Angelis*, set to music by Robert Crane. The eighth note remains constant throughout; a 2-beat pattern should be maintained for the $\frac{4}{8}$ and $\frac{5}{8}$ passages, and a 3-beat pattern for the $\frac{3}{4}$ measures. Remember that smoothness of line is most important in the rendering of a plain chant. The composer has transcribed very sensitively the irregular implications of the rhythm in this famous chant; adhere to them strictly.

KYRIE ELEISON
From *Mass in C*

John Gardner

During the twentieth century there has been renewed interest in ancient chants especially because of their freedom of rhythm. Here is the English composer, John Gardner's Mass in C, which closely resembles Gregorian chant. This is an especially fine exercise for the 1 beat which contains, here, either 2 or 3 eighth notes. There is no discernible pattern of twos and threes to create problems for the conductor, but it makes a beautifully free chant. ($\frac{2}{8} - \frac{3}{8}$ ♪ = 200)

KYRIE
From *Messe*

Paul Hindemith

The *Messe* (1963) was Paul Hindemith's last work and shows the twentieth-century master at his best. It is quite difficult to perform, but these twenty measures from the *Kyrie* have eighth-note patterns, in a contrapuntal texture, which are never too thick for the ear to pick out pitches easily, nor are they too commonplace to challenge the student. A piano should be used to help in rehearsal and will provide a chance for some class members to receive open score-reading practice. The $\frac{9}{8}$, $\frac{8}{8}$, and $\frac{7}{8}$ should be conducted in 3-beat divided patterns, $3 + 3 + 3$, $3 + 3 + 2$ and $3 + 2 + 2$; the $\frac{6}{8}$ of course in a 2-beat pattern.

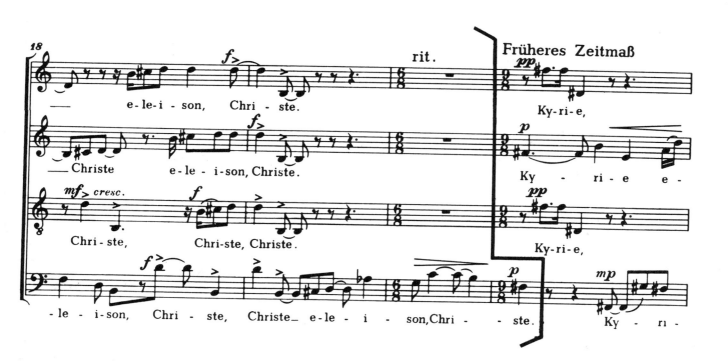

AUTUMN FLOWERS
Music by Gordon Binkerd
Words by Jones Very

Although the eighth note remains constant, there are many conductorial pitfalls in this little excerpt from Gordon Binkerd's *Autumn Flowers*. An excellent opportunity to practice unorthodox eighth-note beat patterns is provided. For instance in the first and eighth measures, $\frac{9}{8}$ falls into a 4-beat pattern 2 + 2 + 3 + 2 which occurs quite frequently in twentieth-century music. The $\frac{7}{8}$ is of course a 3 pattern (2 + 3 + 2), while the $\frac{8}{8}$ is not a subdivided 4, but the usual $\frac{8}{8}$ 3 pattern, here divided 3 + 3 + 2. Follow the dynamics, and keep the eighth notes flowing smoothly.

PSALM 123
Norman Lockwood

The setting of the Psalm 123 by Norman Lockwood presents musical problems for the conductor, which are not solved by beat patterns. The composer commences with a canon that gives the two voices different bar lines. At [A], he writes a descant for the soprano and alto, while the men continue a canonic cycle. A 2 quarter beat pattern is suggested for the opening, starting with an upbeat and a $\frac{4}{4}$ pattern when the parts combine 4 beats before [A]. A 4 beat should be continued, thereafter, until the end. The conductor must emphasize the beats that coincide with the downbeat of the various parts, and he must keep his quarter notes absolutely steady. Visual contact is very important. After the technique of the left hand has been studied, this exercise should be reworked adding left-hand signals.

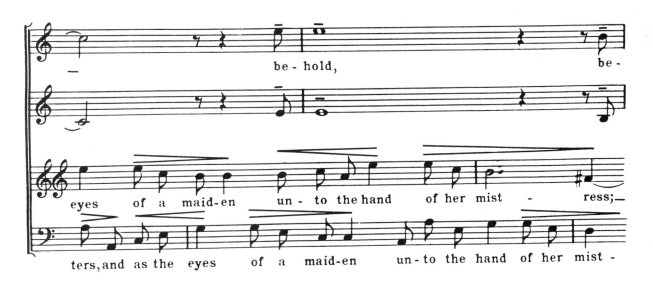

ON VISITING OXFORD
From *A Nation of Cowslips*

Music by Dominick Argento
Words by John Keats

This selection from a choral suite *A Nation of Cowslips* by Dominick Argento is a very difficult piece for the conductor. The difficulty can be easily overcome if the conductor subdivides each half note and makes the ♩ = ♩. , the beat throughout. The half note will, therefore, be conducted as a subdivided beat, equalling ♩ ♪ ♫♫. The composer has employed the medieval technique of planing in the upper two parts, and this is an excellent exercise to train the chorus to hear a perfect fifth.

*Stagger breathing: phrases should be unbroken. Dotted barlines indicate only the co-ordination of high and low voices, not accents.

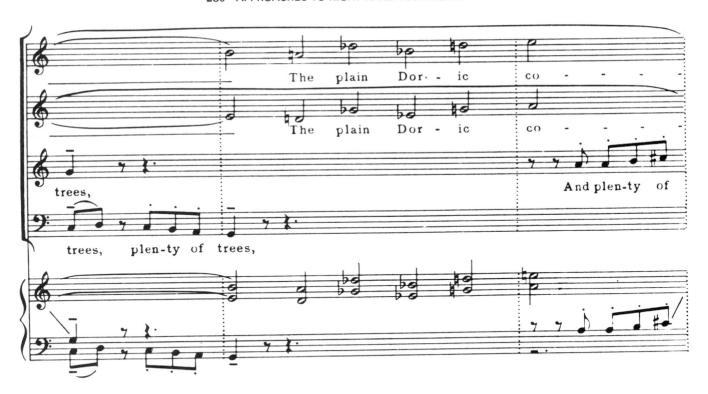

3
Changing Meter Signature with Variable Pulse Symbols

Some of the most perplexing problems confronting the choral conductor in the use of right-hand technique occur when there is a meter change where the number of beats plus the unit of measure change simultaneously such as $\frac{6}{8} - \frac{5}{8} - \frac{3}{4} - \frac{6}{16}$ Usually there is an approximation factor given, for instance ♪. = ♪ or ♩ = ♩. . In these cases it is extremely important that the fastest note in the piece be felt by the conductor. If he feels this, no change in the signature will appreciably upset the flow of music or his "stick" technique.

At this point special attention should be drawn to the "one beat" which was practiced at the beginning of the book and which occurs frequently throughout this chapter. A propitious exercise for practice of the one beat would be any of these:

A "one beat" is of course used at the points marked by the arrows and great care should be taken that the single stroke does last the exact length of 3 or 2 full eighth notes in exercises 1 and 3, and 3 substantial sixteenth notes in exercise 2 without rushing or retarding these measures.

A pertinent subject to discuss at this time even though it relates to music in any rhythm or meter is the problem of breathing. A-rhythmic gaps in the music are often caused by the robbing of a beat or a half beat to replenish breath. This is especially dangerous when rhythmic vitality is essential and there is a change of meters. However, the chorus should be taught that, even in simple $\frac{3}{4}$ meter, a half note normally does not end halfway through the second beat but with the beginning of the third. This becomes very important in a situation that depends on strong rhythmic accents. It is the conductor's duty to work out adequate breathing places and, in cases where there are ostensibly none available (a rare exception), to stagger the breathing within a section so that the vital rhythmic flow is not interrupted.

TO ALL, TO EACH
From *Carols of Death*

Music by William Schuman
Words by Walt Whitman

The first example in this chapter provides a chance to practice a meter change when the "common denominator" is absent. The half note remains a common factor through the changing time signatures at the beginning of William Schuman's "To All to Each," from *Carols of Death*. However, after measure 9 the half note which was at 30 now becomes a dotted half; therefore, the quarter note which equalled 60 at the beginning now equals approximately 90.

‡ Hard "C" of word "Come" should be followed by closed, sustained humming sound.

✱ Tenors divided at conductor's discretion between Alto and Bass parts.
Those Tenors singing Bass line may remain *tacet* during low passages marked in brackets []

GIVE THANKS UNTO THE LORD
Music by Robert Starer

Words from Psalm 136: 1–9

In this anthem, "Give Thanks unto the Lord" by Robert Starer, a straightforward quarter note rhythm is interrupted by a measure or so of 3 eighth notes. The $\frac{3}{8}$ should be conducted in one, but the conductor must make certain that his one beat contains three full eighth notes, and that the rhythm is strengthened, rather than disrupted, by the inclusion of a shortened measure.

IF THAT THE PEACE OF GOD
Warren Benson
Words by Peter Folger

This is an excerpt from a short motet by Warren Benson on words by Peter Folger, who was Benjamin Franklin's grandfather. The tempo is rather gently flowing, and the conductor must make sure that the eighth note remains constant throughout. Though there is no printed indication of a meter change, measure five should be conducted as a $\frac{6}{8}$ rather than a $\frac{3}{4}$ pattern in order to provide a correctly accented rhythm for the prosody. Further, it is suggested that the conductor announce ahead of of time how the $\frac{5}{8}$ and $\frac{7}{8}$ measures are to be divided. Measures 2 and 6 should be 3 + 2, while measures 9 and 13 are divided 2 + 3, and in measure 11 attention must be given to the all important three-eighth note rest at the very beginning, which must be conducted exactly in tempo so as to stabilize the entire piece.

* dotted slur means no breath.

O COME LET US SING
Music by Jean Berger
Words from Psalm 95

Jean Berger's setting of Psalm 95 is another example of a driving, rhythmic choral style. Feel the equal eighth notes throughout, and the subtle, rhythmic accent change between $\frac{3}{4}$, $\frac{6}{8}$, and $\frac{2}{4}$ before rehearsing the passage. Do not choose too fast a tempo for that would destroy the expansiveness of the beginning. A suggested tempo for the first 7 measures is ♩ = 112, and at the marking "Un poco piu mosso" ♩ = 120.

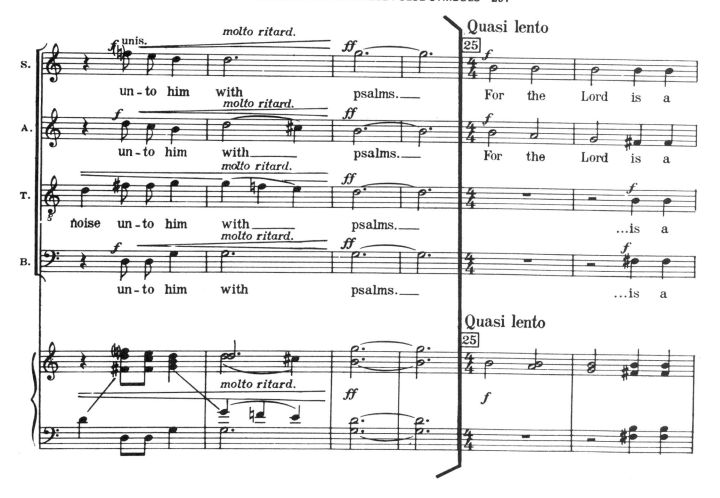

COVENTRY CAROL
Sydney Hodkinson

Words by Robert Croo

Here is an excerpt from the third in a series of eight Christmas carols written by the Canadian-American composer Sydney Hodkinson. It is a wonderful example of easy flowing rhythmic expression of the text, while the meter changes to give the correct accentuation. From the beginning to measure 12, the meter keeps the basic eighth-note pulse, alternating between $\frac{5}{8}$ and $\frac{6}{8}$. Beginning at measure 28, the meter alternates between $\frac{5}{8}$ and $\frac{2}{4}$; nevertheless, the eighth note remains constant, and no change of tempo must occur throughout the entire piece. Hodkinson uses this kind of free-flowing rhythm throughout all of these beautiful carols, and this device gives them a chant-like flavor, truly evocative of Christmas.

SPRING SONG
From *The Lark*

Leonard Bernstein

This is an excerpt from the first of the French choruses that Leonard Bernstein wrote for *The Lark*, adapted by Lillian Hellman from a play by Jean Anouilh. Though the meter changes are not marked, the conductor should conduct this chorus in two distinct patterns in order to accomplish the best rhythmic performance. It falls naturally into $\frac{3}{4}$ followed by $\frac{6}{8}$. Bernstein favors this kind of rhythm in many of his more popular works (*West Side Story*), and here is an example of its use in a semi-sacred work. The excerpt has to be performed in a very rhythmic and "bouncy" way until the composer himself "writes out" a change six measures before the end. During the clapping, be sure to keep the patterns $\frac{3}{4}$ followed by $\frac{6}{8}$, even though the held pitches of the voice parts are seemingly unaffected. The tempo marking is Allegro $\downarrow = 140$, but do not rush the music since the charming rhythm must not suffer from unsteadiness.

MAKE WE JOYE NOWE IN THIS FEST

From *A Christmas Offering*

Music by Gail Kubik

Words Anonymous

The second movement of a work entitled *Christmas Offering*, by Gail Kubik. It is a gay song, with the spirit of a Christmas carol, made more effective by the changes of meter. Be sensitve to the change which occurs between $\frac{2}{4}$ and $\frac{6}{8}$ before you attempt to conduct this excerpt. This little example also offers a good opportunity for "feeling rhythmic rests" in measures 18–19.

WALKING ON THE GREEN GRASS
Michael Hennagin

Here is a most successful little madrigal based on American folk sources. It must be performed with great bounce, and the articulations and changes of meter should be accomplished naturally without ever impeding the flow. It is suggested that the conductor beat four beats to the measure for the first few measures until the tempo is securely set. Thereafter, in order to keep things on the light side, a two (a la breve) beat may be preferable. However, measure 12 should be conducted in a fast two, so that the $\frac{6}{8}$ following can be more easily understood. It is suggested that the $\frac{5}{8}$ measure be divided 2 + 3 and the $\frac{5}{4}$ measure be divided in the same pattern, though the latter could also be conducted 3 + 2 without creating any problems.

GOD, BRING THY SWORD
Music by Ron Nelson
Words by Samuel H. Miller

The beginning of the anthem "God, Bring Thy Sword," by Ron Nelson, also resembles a chant. This is a strong rhythmic declamatory passage with sudden contrasts. The ♪ equals ♪ throughout, which makes the $\frac{6}{4}$ measure rather long. Retain the full value of the eighth notes, for this will emphasize the fast rhythmic declamations more effectively. The $\frac{6}{4}$ may be divided in a 3 pattern, for it is printed as if it were a $\frac{3}{2}$; the eighth and quarter note patterns are very clearly marked throughout.

Optional percussion includes: Tubular chime (♩) sounding ; Snare Drum and Tenor Drum ; High + Low Bongos. Snares are *off* on both drums. Use firm sticks for incisive resonant sound. Never dampen chime.

312

313

PRAYERS OF KIERKEGAARD
Music by Samuel Barber

German translation by Lonja Stehelin-Holzing

Here is an excerpt from Samuel Barber's *Prayers of Kierkegaard* for soprano solo, mixed chorus, and orchestra. Because of the slow tempo, it is suggested that the student give a fast three beat for both $\frac{3}{8}$ measures.

It will emphasize the crescendo, and assure the steadiness of the eighth notes, which remain equal. Use the dynamics fully, and try to build a tremendous climax to the end.

RUSSIAN CREDO
Igor Stravinsky

Besides the large well-known choral works of Stravinsky, there are quite a few smaller ones, written primarily during his early creative period. This is a portion of his *Russian Credo*, to be sung in the original. Become familiar with the rhythm and the notes first before attempting the Russian text. The beat patterns are clear and the ♪ equals a ♪ throughout. $\frac{7}{16}$ is divided 2 + 2 + 3; $\frac{9}{16}$ follows the normal 3 + 3 + 3 division. The meaning of the text is:

I believe in one God, the Father Almighty, Maker of heaven and earth, and of all things visible and invisible.

And in one Lord, Jesus Christ, the only begotten Son of God, begotten of his Father before all worlds. God of God, Light of Light, Very God of Very God, begotten, not made, being of one substance with the Father; by whom all things were made.

IN THE BEGINNING
Music by Aaron Copland

Words from Genesis 1: 1–11: 7

This excerpt is discussed in the appendix of the anthology to show how one would overcome some of the difficulties of rhythm. It is quoted at this time for practice in changing metric patterns, and also to introduce the use of the left hand in giving the "light" signals. Keep your right hand going with the metric flow and use your left for entrances of the different sections at the appropriate time. This is a difficult exercise, but if the student has mastered the previous ones, he should be ready to undertake these new complications. Although meter signatures are not provided, the division of the bars are clearly marked with dotted lines. (The student should add the signatures, if he needs them.) The metronome marking at "Let there be light" is about $\quad = 116$.

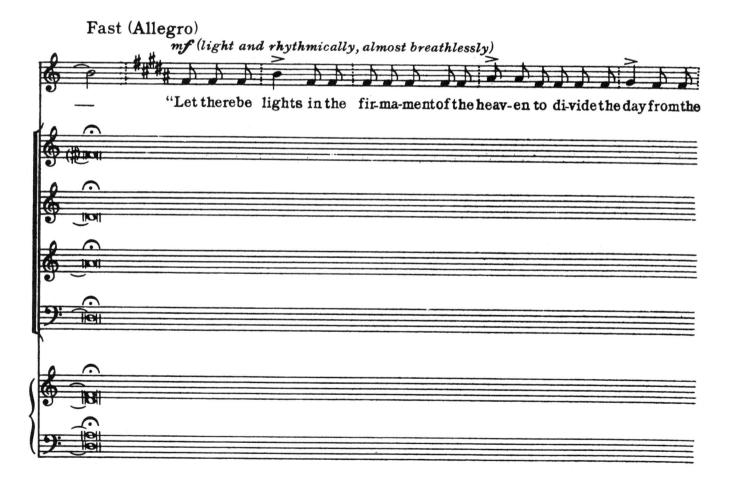

DEVELOPMENT
OF THE
LEFT HAND

4
Cuing

Relatively speaking, it was a simple matter to deal with the problems governing beat patterns and the general assignments given to the right hand of the conductor. The function of the left hand is a different and much more personal and controversial subject.

Most conductors agree that a primary task of the left hand is to give entrance cues during the performance of a piece of music. These entrances must be accomplished while the right hand maintains a steady course with the metric beats. It is to develop such independence of the two hands that a chapter like this one is essential. By and large, the music chosen for this chapter is not of overwhelming difficulty, but if this kind of music is assimilated by the student more intricate passages will be more easily mastered.

Two important points to keep in mind during the utilization of the exercises in this chapter are:

1. The left hand cue for an entrance should be clear and, again, visual contact with the section or sections of the chorus should be made before the gesture is executed.

2. The nature of the left hand motion should certainly be governed by the musical content of the passage. If this sounds redundant, it is meant to be: this fact cannot be overemphasized. The student should practice "throwing" cues in all directions during fast, slow, loud, and soft passages. Each condition should evoke a slightly different left-hand motion toward the

particular choral section cued. This motion would convey by its character the musical feeling of the particular moment at which it is given. Quick, off-beat entrances are especially tricky and should be studied closely. (Bach's "Christ Lag in Todesbanden").

Here the problem of "overconducting" arises. Keep a steady beat and practice the left hand cuing of off-beat entrances without subdividing the beats. However, it cannot be stressed enough in such situations that the inner beat must be felt strongly by both conductor as well as chorus so that the division of the beat into any apportionment will be relatively easy and natural. One other hint in studying entrance problems: it is imperative to know exactly who comes in when. Understanding of the music being conducted has been stressed throughout the comments in this anthology. Nowhere is this more important than in the problem of cuing.

CANTATE DOMINO
Heinrich Schütz

English version adapted by Lowell P. Beveridge
from the Book of Common Prayer

Here is an excerpt from a popular but quite difficult motet of Heinrich Schütz (1585–1672). Clarity is the most important factor in determining speed, and it may be necessary to conduct the piece in a fast three, though the feeling should be in one. The common musicological wisdom today is divided as to whether Baroque music should be performed faster than was customary in the last century and up to 1950. While experts debate over this performance practice, it is suggested that the clarity and precision of the eighth-note runs finally determine the speed. Cuing is a great problem at the beginning of the motet since the entrances are so close together. It is really not necessary during a performance to give these rapid entrances, but in rehearsal, and especially in conducting practice sessions, it would be beneficial for the conductor to see if he can cue all the entrances with his left hand or with a combination of hands and eyes. It is a great little excerpt to practice one's cuing skills. Do not forget that the dynamics and expression marks are those of an editor and should be largely disregarded. The piece should be performed at a rather loud dynamic and "calm down" naturally during the final five measures quoted here. As regards tempo, the metronome marking is simply a suggestion; as long as the piece exudes joy and happiness in performance, the tempo is correct.

TO MUSIC
Music by Elliott Carter

Words by Robert Herrick

It is unfortunate that Elliot Carter, one of the most distinguished American composers, has written so little for chorus. There are only a few early pieces; "To Music" is one of them. This is a linear piece, and the left hand should be assigned the task of pointing out the important lines, by giving the chorus clear entrance indications. The signal should be given even when there is no great pause before re-entry. The tempo must not be rushed, for there are many words to sing on short notes. ♩ = 76 is the suggested speed. Observe all dynamic marks. The excerpt is in 4/4.

AND WITH HIS STRIPES
From *Messiah*

Georg Friedrich Handel

This well-known chorus from Handel's *Messiah* presents real problems in cuing: first, because there are so many entrances to be cued; second, because there are so many different articulations. The subject of the fugue should have breadth and majesty, while the separate quarter notes should "bounce" a bit to give contrast, and the slurred passages must be very smooth and flowing. This chorus is unique because it is one of the few examples of a completely developed choral fugue by Handel. Therefore, it always seems one of the most difficult choruses to perform in *Messiah* but also one of the most rewarding and satisfying.

HANUKKAH
From *Six Madrigals*

by Herbert Fromm

The last repeat of the refrain from " 'Hanukkah' Madrigal" by Herbert Fromm. The piece is based on a traditional melody to celebrate the Jewish Feast of Lights. It resembles a sixteenth-century madrigal and should be sprightly. The entrances are easy to signal, and the left hand should be active in reducing the volume for the piano entrances and effecting the retard at the end. The metronome marking is ♪ = 140. (Begin at arrow.)

KYRIE
From *Requiem*

Wolfgang Amadeus Mozart

It is difficult to find a point at which to cut off this great double fugue, which ends the first chorus of the Mozart *Requiem*. There is ample opportunity for the left hand to signal two different kinds of entrances here, for the structure of the two themes is very different. One variety is stately, while the other is lively and includes ornamental figures. The cue gesture must indicate the exact mood and feeling to the entering section. Avoid a big retard leading to the diminished seventh chord, which occurs three measures before the end, but provide an exciting, sensational climax; maintain the tension by using the cutoff as the rest, and sustaining a continuous rhythmic drive to the shocking open chord at the end. M.M. ♩ = 108.

OMNES GENERATIONES
From *Magnificat*

Johann Sebastian Bach

The left hand plays an important part in the entrance pattern of the stirring chorus "Omnes generationes " from Bach's *Magnificat*. There is no relaxation in either drive or dynamics, and any experimentation with effects would be inadvisable. There is a new trend for choral conductors to over-interpret such excerpts and use them for emoting; however, the music speaks for itself. The conductor's big job is to maintain the vitality of the tempo and rhythm, the accuracy of the notes, and understand the contrapuntal workings of the piece.

363

364

365

5

The Left Hand
as a Dynamics
and Expression Guide

The previous chapter discussed the only task of the left hand about which almost all conductors and students of conducting will agree: the giving of cues, especially in cases where the entrance of a voice does not coincide with the continuing beat pattern. This chapter concerns itself with some nebulous questions and controversial issues related to the use of the left hand.

A second function of the left hand is to aid the right hand in clarifying and communicating even more extensively the will and intention of the conductor. The right hand expresses the metric flow of the music; the left hand communicates the conductor's emotional and psychological thoughts about the work. This statement has brought about the fallacious idea that the left hand is used predominantly for "emoting." Not at all. However, the use of the left hand initiates perhaps the final refinement in communication between the conductor and his organization.

Some of the more obvious technical functions of the left hand are:

1. To indicate volume (loud, soft, louder, softer).

2. To give warning of sudden changes in tempo or dynamics, and reinforce crescendo, diminuendo, ritardando, and accellerando passages.

3. To emphasize an accented beat or an important phrasing consideration.

4. To support the dynamism and precision of the beat in particularly complicated, rhythmic passages. This is a subjective matter; however, the

involvement of both hands on heavily stressed rhythmic accents tends to add to the steadiness of the execution of difficult passages containing changes. This remark should not be misconstrued as an endorsement of perpetual left-hand duplication of the right-hand beat pattern; this would be absurd. Left-hand movement in this context should add emphasis to a few important beats and last only a short period of time. Furthermore, mirroring of the right hand by the left tends to obscure the beat.

Without becoming dogmatic, the student and teacher should come to some sort of understanding about (1) the position of the left hand when it is not in use, and (2) the independence of the left hand while it is in use. Too often, while witnessing a performance, one is made aware that the conductor is inept, because of the awkward, almost frustrated, use of his left hand. The suggestions made in this chapter are extremely important as a first step in the development of an independent, natural use of the left hand.

The following exercises should be practiced repeatedly, with emphasis on the involvement of the left hand. Work on the beat patterns first; then add the following tasks, executing them with the left hand.

1. Crescendo and diminuendo indications on certain predetermined beats or measures.

2. Ritardandos and accellerandos indicated over a two or three measure pattern.

3. Entrances given by the left hand, especially off the beat, should be reviewed and restudied.

4. Conduct the following exercises using the left hand to help the right mark the given accents more clearly. The left hand is only to be used on notes indicated by an arrow.

Sing each pattern note on "ta" while conducting.

Suggested pieces to be redone with emphasis on left-hand expressive motions

Chapter 1
    Liebeslieder Walzer, Opus 52
    Jack der Spratt
    O Vos Omnes Qui Transistis Per Viam
    Yver, vous nestes qu'un villain
    Fire, Fire My Heart
    The Shepherds' Farewell
    Laudate Dominum
    April Is in My Mistress' Face
    Three Rounds in $\frac{4}{4}$ Time
    He That Shall Endure to the End
    Lo Country Sports
    Sixth Madrigal
Chapter 2
    God's Time Is the Best
    Bless Ye the Lord
    Lament
    Kyrie (from *Messe*)
    Psalm 123
    On Visiting Oxford
Chapter 3
    Spring Song
    Walking on the Green Grass
    Prayers of Kierkegaard
    In the Beginning

CALIGAVERUNT OCULI MEI
Music by Tomás Luis de Victoria

Arranged by Peter J. Wilhousky

Tomás Luis de Victoria (1549–1611) was the greatest of all Spanish court composers. There is a possibility that his teacher may have been Palestrina, but in any case, he was Palestrina's successor at the Roman Seminary in 1571. This very beautiful and popular a cappella piece is included here to let the left hand help interpret and practice giving an entrance cue that by its characteric motion will suggest a soft dynamic. The dynamic markings are the editor's, and they may be altered in any way that may be suitable. Furthermore, there is some question as to the editor's choice of tempo.

♩ = 72 seems much too fast and it would seem advisable to keep it closer to ♩ = 80, even though the breve sign is present. This does not mean a really fast tempo. It should be tried both ways before a decision is reached.

MOURN, YE AFFLICTED CHILDREN
From *Judas Maccabaeus*

G. F. Handel

Words by the Rev. Thos. Morell, D. D.

It is unfortunate that since "The Messiah" is so well suited to a particular holiday, it is the only oratorio of Handel's that is well known to all; many of the others contain equally stirring moments. The oratorios referred to especially are *Israel in Egypt, Solomon, Saul,* and *Judas Maccabaeus.* This is the first chorus from *Judas Maccabaeus.* The heavy and "afflicted" quality should be mirrored by the performance. It is suggested that a divided beat be given for a short time, and once all parts feel the eighth notes, a regular four beat will suffice. The left hand is essential, not only for entrances, but for the expression marks as well. A good tempo would be ♪ = 80.

sol - - emn strains, mourn, — your fa-ther, your

mourn in sol - emn strains, your he-ro, your fa-ther, mourn, — your

sol - - emn strains, your he-ro, mourn, — your he-ro is no

sol - - emn strains, your he-ro, your fa-ther, your he-ro is no

he - ro is no more, your fa-ther is no more, your fa-ther

he - ro is no more, your fa-ther is no more, your fa-ther

more, your fa-ther is no more, mourn, your fa-ther

more, your fa-ther is no more, mourn, your fa-ther

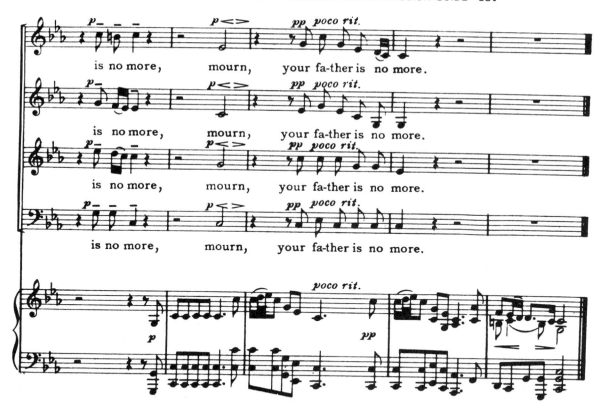

HE, WATCHING OVER ISRAEL

From *Elijah*

Felix Mendelsshon

This is probably one of the best known choruses from Mendelssohn's *Elijah*, but one that is often presented badly. The job of the left hand is to warn the singers of difficulties and to stop them from overdoing effects. The first pitfall is in the first melodic line. More often than not the interval A to F♯ is sung with such a large crescendo by both soprano and tenor that the whole mood is destroyed. The next danger spot is the second melody on the word "grief." It is true that there is an emotional impact to the phrase, but the sf must be natural and not forced in order to prevent the next appogiatura from sounding like an afterthought. These are all labors for an expressive left hand. Keep the tempo alive and make no retards anywhere in this example.

HOW LOVELY IS THY DWELLING PLACE
From *Requiem*

Johannes Brahms

Another choral mainstay, the fifth movement from the Brahms' *Requiem*. However, the student should cherish the idea of giving a new and personal interpretation to old masterpieces. The excerpt is included for this reason, and also because the work of the left hand is certainly very important here. Attention should be paid to the crescendo at the phrase "dwell that dwell within thy house." A phrase of this kind separates the good from the mediocre conductors. Excitement should spring forth during this passage which will lead naturally into the fugato. One cannot help picking up the tempo during this climactic passage, but then it is the duty of the conductor to return significantly to the beginning tempo at D. It would be advisable to try a slight diminuendo for two or three measures to four measures before D, and then make an almost subito piano on "evermore." Then experiment with a gradual piano. This excerpt should give many opportunities to the left hand for expression.

AVE MARIA
Anton Bruckner

Anton Bruckner is often revered only for his symphonies which, though great contributions to the literature, are certainly rivaled by his choral music. There is much sacred choral music by this late nineteenth-century German master, culminating perhaps with the large Mass in e minor. In 1860 Bruckner became conductor of a choral group called "Frohsinn" Society and wrote several shorter a cappella works for them. The first of these shorter pieces was this "Ave Maria," premiered in 1861 and a favorite ever since. The tempo is marked *Andante* and in parenthesis "very slow." One cannot be sure exactly what this means, since Andante itself should not be interpreted as "very slow" but rather "gently moving." Frankly, if the piece is taken too slowly, it can drag terribly; it is therefore suggested that it be conducted rather flexibly so that each phrase will come out most expressively. The left hand should be used to bring out the many expression marks called for by the composer, and of course to bring in new voices as they enter. It is a short but volatile piece in which good use of a steady right hand and an expressive and agile left hand are necessary to assure a successful performance.

SPECIAL
CHORAL
PROBLEMS

6
Coping
with
Accompaniments

The most obvious complication that arises with the inclusion of an independent accompaniment in choral music is that with the increase of forces an added musical consideration enters the picture. Much of what we have discussed so far takes on additional importance: especially the conductor's need for clarity, precision, and absolute assurance in his knowledge of the music which now must include an independent accompaniment. Even if this accompaniment is simply a piano or a single instrument such as a violin, viola, or cello, the conductor, except for cadenzas, should never cease beating so that both chorus and accompaniment feel the rhythm constantly. This chapter contains examples of the chorus being accompanied as well as the chorus acting as an accompanying agent to a soloist. In addition, a few examples of purely orchestral passages are included for study. These should be conducted first while they are played on the piano and recordings should be used only after they are mastered. Of course if the student is fortunate enough to have an instrumental group at his disposal, this is preferable to all other alternatives. Notwithstanding a desire to avoid a dogmatic viewpoint, it is urged that a baton be used for conducting when the accompaniment calls for instruments other than the piano. This is a matter of custom as well as one of clarity and ease in communication, since usually the addition of instruments spreads the ensemble further apart and away from the conductor. The baton should be considered as an extension of the hand or arm of the conductor.[1]

When any independent accompaniment is present the following thoughts are pertinent and must be considered:

1. Be especially aware of the problems of balance between soloist and chorus as well as between the accompaniment and the chorus. Many works are overscored and the soloist or the chorus may easily be drowned out. When a vocal soloist is present remember that his or her timbre mixes very easily with the sound of the chorus and, if the balance is not judiciously maintained, may be overshadowed by the mass. Always consider diligently the implications of the register in which the soloist is singing and gear the strength of the choral accompaniment accordingly. This applies conversely to the chorus when an orchestra is present, for an orchestra can easily overwhelm a chorus, and therefore the tessitura as well as the dynamics must play a determining role in the conductor's balancing decisions.

2. A soloist is an independent human interpreter; therefore tempi and liberties in the interpretation of the music should be agreed upon ahead of time. The beat must be flexible to accommodate some of the wishes of the soloist without distorting the musical content appreciably. A conductor accompanying any soloist should always be prepared for unexpected "bends" in the rhythmic flow caused by emotional considerations or tensions occurring during a performance. Perfect knowledge of the solo part cannot be overemphasized.

3. Special care should be exercised to see that entrances of the chorus, the soloists, or the instrumental group are well coordinated. In fast passages which lead to vocal entrances, be sure to concentrate on certain notes or phrases that will aid in "catching" the soloist, in order to produce a smooth group entrance. This is especially difficult after a cadenza. Visual contact between conductor and soloists again becomes a most crucial concern.

4. Another vital consideration is the placement of the soloists vis-à-vis the chorus or the placement of chorus, soloists, and accompanying group. One precept should govern all considerations: all participants must be able to watch the conductor with perfect ease while performing.

[1] For a rather controversial discussion of this subject refer to Chapter IV of Brock McElheran's book "Conducting Technique," New York: Oxford University Press, 1966.

PSALM: "ALL PRAISE TO HIM"

From *King David*

Music by Arthur Honegger

Words by Rene Morax

We begin this chapter with a somewhat simple excerpt from Arthur Honegger's oratorio *King David.* This rather Baroque setting of words from Psalms presents a two-part (chorus and bass) structure; each part is equally important and has a similar rhythmic impetus, while the trumpet interrupts with a scale passage. The accompaniment should be unimpeded by the cessation of the chorus part, and must proceed smoothly to the end. Do not retard the last phrase of the chorus, and make sure that the triumphant and joyous spirit prevails throughout, with an absolutely steady beat.

pealed on the heads of the foe, Who in their ma - lice sought my___ end.

LIBERA ME
From *Requiem*

Giuseppe Verdi

Another easily conducted passage; this time from Verdi's *Requiem*. However, because of the extreme dynamics great skill should be exercised (especially in the entrances of the chorus) not to jar the smoothness and sublime lyricism of the solo line. The left hand should be of great assistance in creating the subtle crescendi and diminuendi indicated in the score, as well as aiding in entrances and phrasing considerations throughout the piece. It goes without saying that in all excerpts of this kind the co-ordination between soloist and chorus is essential, and the conductor must give some leeway for the soprano to "express" herself.

GLORIA
From *Misa Criolla*

Ariel Ramírez

This is a short quotation from the *Misa Criolla* by Ariel Ramírez. It contains Latin rhythms and is accompanied by piano (harpsichord), percussion, and bass. The instruments are essential to the performance of the piece; therefore, if the exact instruments are not available, some should be improvised, so that the conductor will have the opportunity to feel the different rhythms, and a chance to give cues to all concerned. The reason for the strange printing of the chords at the beginning (even though the rhythm is the same in both hands) is to achieve the effect of a "broken chord," with the lower two notes slightly anticipating the notes in the right hand.

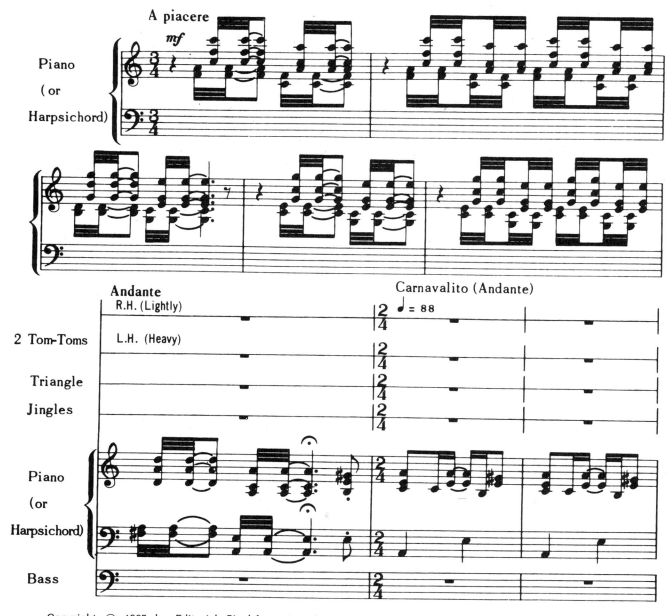

405

O CLAP YOUR HANDS
Ralph Vaughan Williams
from Psalm 47

The text comes from Psalm 47 and is set for brass septet, percussion, and organ. This is a brief work that makes a powerful musical statement. This excerpt is the very end of the piece and, because of its brevity, it is most important that there be a truly gradual build-up to the Allegro Molto. Take the Lento quite slowly and rhythmically vital; then pace the Andante quite broadly with an accellerando over the four measures just before the Allegro. This Allegro should be conducted in three also, but of course with the beat much faster, leading *subito* into the Allegro Molto in one. The piece ends with a "written out" ritard, and it is suggested that only at the very end (the last three measures of the brass) should an actual slowing take place, possibly beating the final two bars in three. If at all possible, the piece should be practiced with brass instruments so that the conductor may experience the feeling of coordinating the chorus with the instruments and making certain the beat is absolutely clear for both forces.

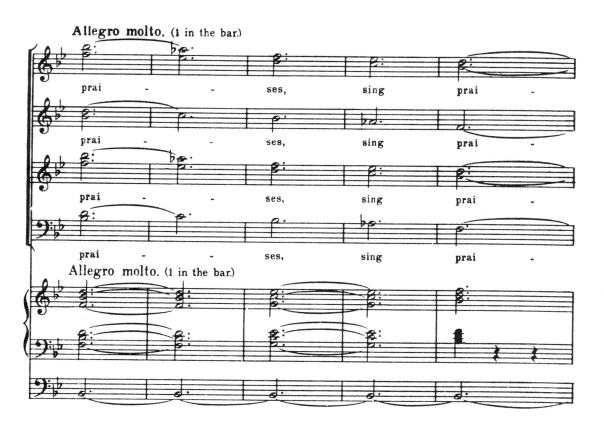

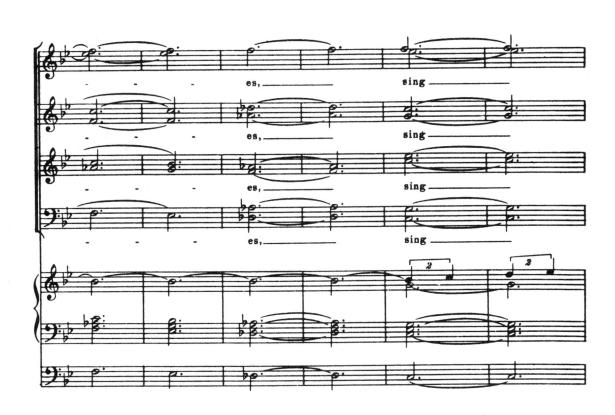

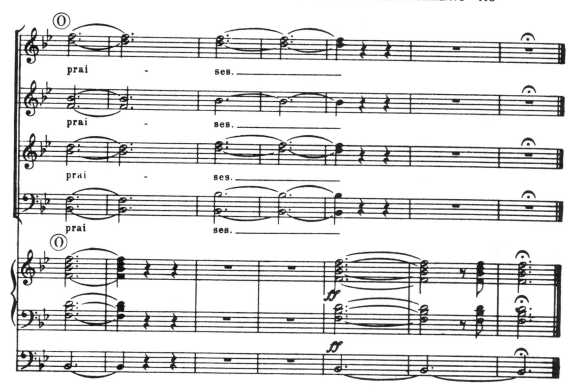

ADONOY YIMLOCH
From Sacred Service

Ernst Bloch

The *Sacred Service* of Ernst Bloch (1880–1959) has become one of the favorite twentieth-century collaborations between chorus and orchestra. It is a powerful expression of the Jewish Sabbath liturgy and the first version of this collection of prayers ever scored for chorus and orchestra. Many composers in our century have followed Bloch's example: Milhaud, Fromm, Berlinsky, Ben Haim, Yeheskel Braun, as well as this author, have composed music for chorus and orchestra inspired by this service. The excerpt here presents the conductor with a special problem because of the dichotomy between the articulation of the chorus and that of the accompaniment. For the first nine measures after 21, the accompaniment "opposes" the rhythmic "squareness" of the chorus, and there is often quite a bit of uncertainty in performance until the downbeat of measure seven is reached. One way to solve the problem is let the chorus hear the accompaniment first, and then fit the chorus into it. Be sure the downbeat at 21, as well as on each measure thereafter, is very clear so that the momentary instability that the composer intended will merge easily and naturally into the martial triumph of the rest of the piece.

SYMPHONY OF PSALMS
(A) CHORAL
Igor Stravinsky

The *Symphony of Psalms* by Igor Stravinsky is considered one of the masterpieces of choral music of the twentieth century. An excerpt from the beginning is quoted here to show the great importance of the orchestral accompaniment, and the difference between the character of the choral part and the instrumental portion. This difference must manifest itself through the beat, as well as the "instructions" by means of signals given in the use of the left hand. It is suggested that the right hand "conduct" the orchestra, while the left hand "dictate" the choral part. Naturally the tempo and spirit should be similar, but, also, the emotional quality is emphasized by this procedure.

SYMPHONY OF PSALMS
(B) ORCHESTRA

Igor Stravinsky

421

UF DEM ANGER
(A) CHORAL
From *Carmina Burana*

Carl Orff

Carl Orff's "Carmina Burana" has become a very popular piece for collaboration between college choruses and symphony orchestras throughout the country. The choral portions of the work present few major conducting challenges, but this little orchestral excerpt is a bit tricky rhythmically and rather finicky in its subtle tempo changes. Here, as in all examples involving orchestral accompaniment, the use of piano is strongly recommended, until the student has mastered the piece. Then a recording should be used. If possible several different recordings should be played to illustrate the diverse ways in which a piece can be approached.

UF DEM ANGER
(B) ORCHESTRA
From *Carmina Burana*

Carl Orff

6. Tanz

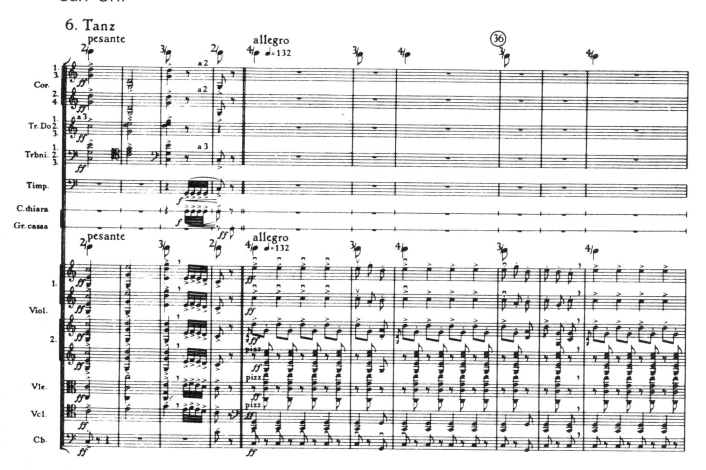

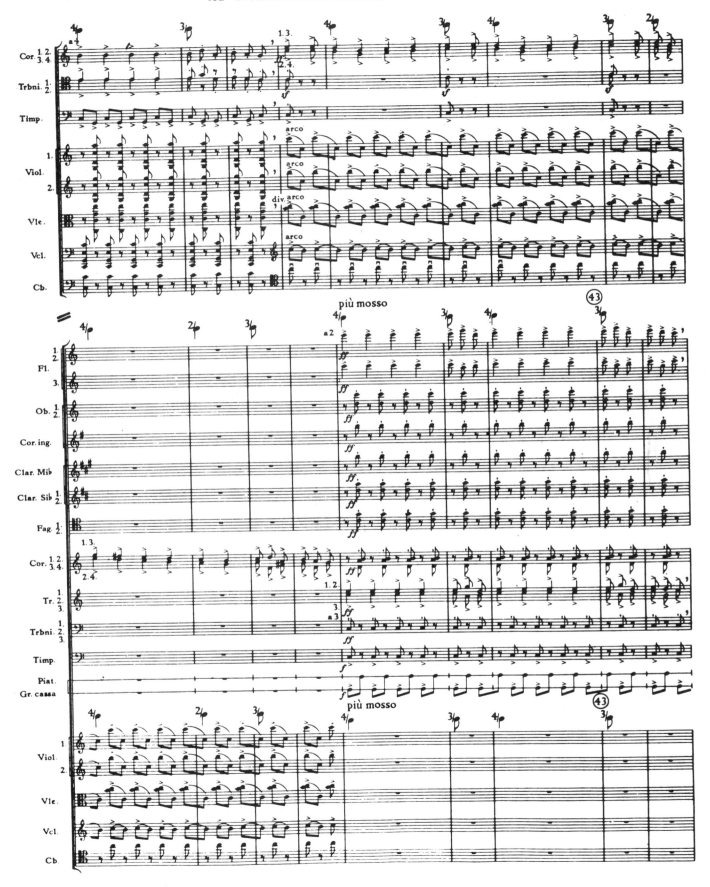

BELSHAZZAR'S FEAST
William Walton

Certainly, another outstanding extended choral work of this century is William Walton's *Belshazzar's Feast.* In this excerpt the composer is representing ancient Babylon and the orgy which was being celebrated in the palace of Belshazzar before the famous "handwriting on the wall" disrupted pagan festivities. Walton draws the picture with exquisite orchestration and powerful, revelling music, which should have tremendous drive, rhythmic exactness, and rhythmic vitality in both choral and orchestral parts. Be certain that the eighth notes remain constant, and that the tempo does not "sag" at the words, "and his concubines." Here the chorus is more lyric and without the orchestral drive; nevertheless, the tension must be maintained. M.M. ♩ = 126.

PSALM 57
Jean Berger

Jean Berger is very well known for his a cappella and organ accompanied works; however, he has quite a few works for chorus with non-keyboard, instrumental accompaniments. This is an excerpt from one of these pieces—the beginning of "Psalm 57." It is quoted here because of the rhythmic intricacies of the accompanying brass parts. It also offers a good opportunity to restate the purpose of this chapter. The fact that a choral conductor must be able to conduct the instrumental portions of a work, as well as, if not even more knowledgeably than the choral portions, cannot be emphasized enough. Here the $\frac{10}{8}$ should be conducted in a 4 (3 + 2 + 2 + 3) and the $\frac{8}{8}$ in 3 (3 + 3 + 2). All the other signature patterns are clearly indicated by the barring of the notes.

Be mer-ci-ful_un-to me, O God, be mer-ci-ful_un-to me:

Be mer-ci-ful_un-to me, O God, be mer-ci-ful_un-to me:

FESTIVAL TE DEUM
Benjamin Britten

The beautiful beginning of Benjamin Britten's *Festival Te Deum* is very difficult to conduct because of the problem of coordination between vocal and organ parts. The composer has provided small notes to indicate to the organist, and of course to the conductor, where the ostinato chord rhythm occurs. The simplest solution for the conductor would be to disregard the organist and let him fend for himself. A new and different problem would be created for the student if the right hand were assigned the task of conducting the chorus, while the left hand indicated to the organist when he is to play the chord.

* The appogiaturas to be played quickly (but distinctly) and *on* the beat.

✦ The small notes between the staves of the organ part indicate the rhythm of the Choir.

BY THE RIVERS OF BABYLON
Music by David Amram

Psalm 137

The ending of the anthem "By the Rivers of Babylon" by David Amram, with words from Psalm 137, gives the conducting student the opportunity to balance a soprano soloist against four other female parts. The music is rather simple and does not present any insurmountable rhythmic or vocal problems, but the timbre of the voices must be well modulated to let the soloist come through without having to "push." The composer has solved some of this problem by careful spacing. The tempo for the first measure is Tempo I which is ♪ = 96.

AN DIE FREUDE
From *Symphony No. 9*

Ludwig van Beethoven

Very few of us are ever fortunate enough to conduct Beethoven's Ninth Symphony, but many choral conductors are called upon to prepare the chorus for this magnificent work. Here is the "mock-war" section with tenor soloist and male chorus. I quote from measures 358 through 431 of the finale. Be certain that the pseudo-march jagged flavor always comes through even in the more lyrical choral or solo passages. No adequate solo tenor may be available, but for practice purposes perhaps a soprano or two may be substituted. If no one is able to realize the part, it may be necessary to revert to a second piano. A tenor is, of course, preferable. Translation:

Glad as suns that He hurtles
Through the vast spaces of heaven,
Pursue your pathway, brothers;
Be joyful as a hero in victory.

PSALM 112

No. 8

Georg Friedrich Handel

There are many Psalm settings by Handel, including a body of Psalm Cantatas called *Chandos Anthems*. This Psalm 112 is from a collection of Latin Psalm settings. The end of the Psalm is quoted, with the "non-Psalm" words, "As it was in the beginning is now and ever shall be world without end, Amen." Here both chorus and orchestra act as an accompaniment for the soprano soloist. This excerpt is included to exemplify the frequent occurrence of this texture and style of writing in the Baroque, Classical, and early Romantic periods. Coordination, dynamics, steady rhythmic drive, ornamental and linear problems are all contained in this powerful excerpt ($\quad$ = 180).

SET DOWN SERVANT
Arranged by Robert Shaw

Robert Shaw's arrangement of the black spiritual "Set Down Servant" must be one of the all-time favorite pieces in this genre. Yet the problem of coordination encountered in the accompaniment of the soloist by the humming and "doodling" chorus is not often surmounted successfully. The singer must be free to "emote," while the conductor has his chorus so well under control that he can signal the start of a new phrase easily and make it all sound very natural. The tempo at Ⓑ is slow and quite "free," though the soloist should follow the notated rhythm as closely as possible. Then suddenly at the "a tempo," the chorus must snap into the original tempo of ♩ = 92 − 100. Why it is marked $\frac{4}{4}$ instead of ¢, which occurs two measures later, is a mystery since the music suggests that the tempo remains the same. Go straight into an *alla breve* beat at "a tempo" and keep the fast tempo all the way to the upbeat of the final two measures, where a slow four beat takes hold to the very end. The final pages (from Ⓒ) must have the greatest intensity and must drive to the end with a charging kind of ecstasy.

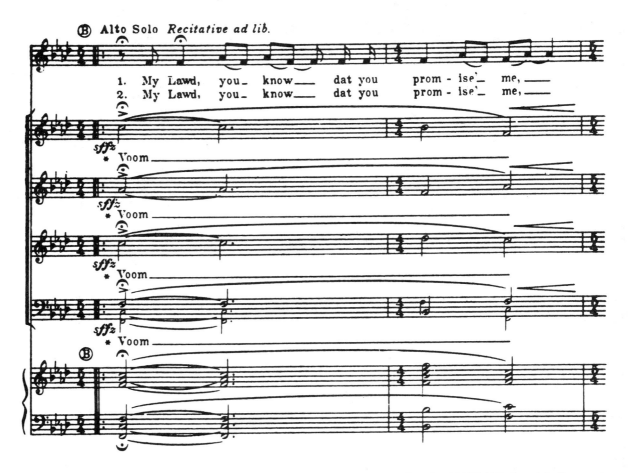

"Prom-ise' me a long white robe — An' a pair___ of shoes."
"Prom-ise' me a long white robe — An' a gold - en waist band."

Voom _____ Voom oo

Voom _____ Voom oo

Voom _____ Voom

Voom _____ Voom

* Close to hum immediately.

Bass Solo (or Baritone *8va*) *Recitative ad lib.*

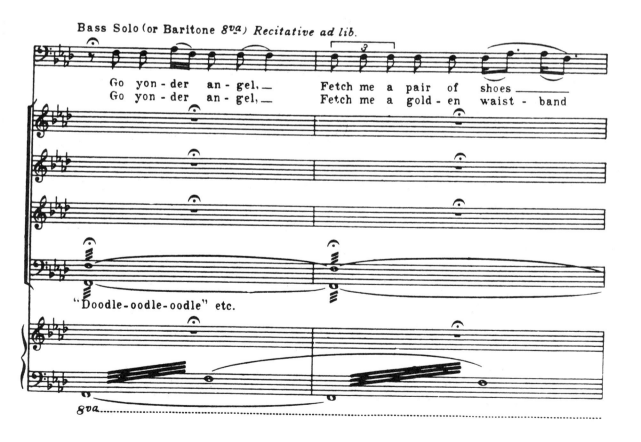

Go yon - der an - gel, — Fetch me a pair of shoes ___
Go yon - der an - gel, — Fetch me a gold - en waist - band

"Doodle - oodle - oodle" etc.

8va..

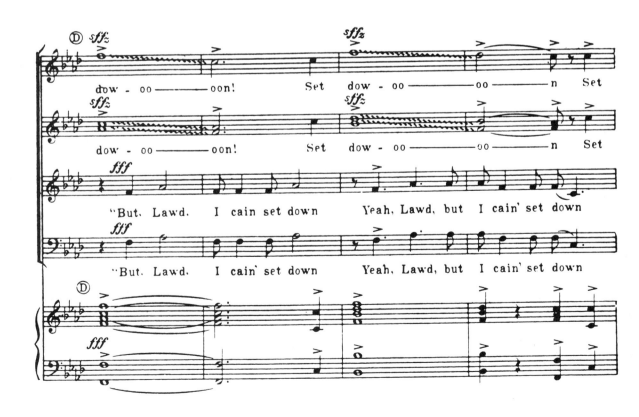

ALTO RHAPSODIE
Johannes Brahms

Here is an excerpt from one of Brahms's most romantic works for alto solo, male chorus, and orchestra. Because of this combination it is not as frequently performed as the mixed chorus works; nevertheless, it deserves the attention of students of choral conducting. The tempo of these final pages, as of most of the work, is slow (Adagio) and stately without any feeling of dragging. The triplets in the orchestra should keep a constant heavy but forward-moving feeling, and one must sense an underlying quiet exuberance. The "conflict" between the triplets in the accompaniment and the duplets in the chorus is typically Brahmsian, and a special effort must be made to keep these two elements steady. The chorus as well as the orchestral parts must be conducted flexibly so that the soloist has room for a bit of *rubata* in her interpretation. Do not make any ritard at the end, for Brahms "writes it out," and the ending would be destroyed if artificially lengthened. In a class presentation for the purposes of practicing conducting, the tenor parts may be supported or taken over wholly by women, of course singing an octave lower "at pitch."

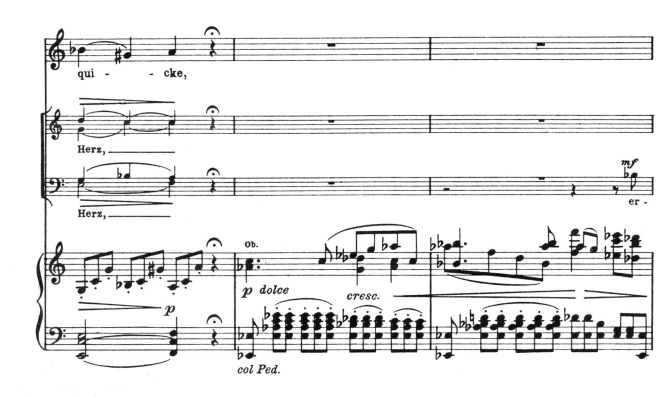

qui - - - cke   sein Herz!

qui - - - cke   sein Herz!

SURELY HE HATH BORNE OUR GRIEFS
From *Messiah*

Georg Friedrich Handel

The second excerpt from Handel's *Messiah* is very famous, and is quoted in many books on choral conducting because of the dichotomy in feeling between portions of the accompaniment and the choral parts. Only one bit of advice can be offered here: the dotted rhythm must persuade the conductor that intensity and tension are present and vitalize all the other notes, whether they are held quarters and eighth notes, or equal sixteenth notes. In other words, the inner beat will make or break this composition. A divided four pattern is essential, and special care must be taken not to obscure the downbeat by this division. A word of caution about the middle section after the dotted rhythm stops: even though the "drive" should give way to a little relaxation, the harmonic intensity must be brought out and should not let the tension erode nor the tempo slow down. Then lead, very naturally, back to the feeling of the beginning.

Isaiah liii: **4, 5**

Largo e staccato (♪ = 72)

Piano

*) Many editions have 𝆑 ≡ here; according to Händel's score, 𝑔 is correct.

A LINCOLN LETTER
Ulysses Kay

Here we have the final few pages from Ulysses Kay's *A Lincoln Letter*, a short a cappella work for baritone and chorus. Balance and coordination are the conductor's chief problems, although the composer provides the soloist with an extremely advantageous range, so that he may cut through the chorus. The dynamics are also very explicit and must be strictly observed if the soloist is to prevail. A word about the tempo: keep the eighth notes moving along, but gear the tempo to the words so that these will come out very clearly and without being rushed by the set tempo. The metronome marking is ♩ = 116.

PSALMS
Part 2

Lukas Foss

This excerpt comes from Part II of *Psalms* by Lukas Foss. The work was originally scored for mixed chorus and two pianos, but an orchestral accompaniment is available. The words of this particular passage are taken from Psalm 98. Measures 203 to 251 are quoted and are an episode in a rather extended fugal section at a fast tempo (♩ = 132 — 138). At this tempo the fitting of voices with the two pianos becomes quite difficult, and the balancing of the incidental tenor soloist presents an added problem. This is a wonderfully exuberant passage and the crisp playing of the piano parts must be complemented by staccato choral passages of the greatest rhythmic accuracy in order to establish the desired effect.

BENEDICTUS

From *Mass in G Minor*

Ralph Vaughan Williams

The "Benedictus" from Ralph Vaughan Williams' *Mass in G* is quoted here to give the student the opportunity to handle large vocal forces. There are four soloists and two choruses to be considered. Coordination and entrance problems are essential in this beautiful excerpt, and the subtle piano shadings should be carefully studied so that the sudden forte "Osannahs" will be even more effective in contrast. The tempo of the "Benedictus" is quite slow: ♩ = 60 is suggested, with a picking up the tempo at "Osannah II" to ♩ = ca. 69.

490

Osanna II

7
Dealing
with
Aural Complexities

The problems dealt with in this anthology are not separate entities. Because we have first discussed dexterity problems should not diminish the importance given to other aspects inherent in the art of proficient conducting. The conductor and the composer are perhaps the greatest embodiment or synthesis of all musical skills and traits. The attributes discussed separately throughout this anthology must of course merge in the person of the conductor naturally and automatically. His ear and ability to hear not only the notes but the rhythm, the timbre, and control the over-all psychological impact of a performance are fundamental to all conductorial considerations.

Hopefully, while conducting all the exercises thus far in the anthology, the student has paid close attention to the accuracy of the notes, the conciseness of the rhythm, as well as the precision of the intonation. In the twentieth century some of these factors have been complicated by new compositional techniques which tax the ear even more than the problems faced in precontemporary times. Not only must the conductor be conscious of one key at a time, of tonality, of a "fitting" vocal line, but today of non-tonality, bitonality and polytonality. Serial writing and improvisation form a vital and fascinating contribution to the outstanding choral repertoire.

These exercises should be taken seriously and studied thoroughly. The reason for keeping many of them short is that each student should be given a chance to preside over their realization. If they are to be performed a cappella, an instrument should be utilized until the sound is firmly embedded in the ear, and exercises should be created by the student following the general patterns of the passages themselves, devised to further challenge and educate the ear to "new" sounds. Quotation marks are around the word "new," for as soon as a sound or a compositional technique is used today for the first time, it is no longer new. The 12-tone technique has been practiced for over fifty years now, yet too many people, especially performers, are still unaware of its existence and of the tremendous repertoire that exists utilizing this compositional principle. The same may be said of other contemporary techniques. Curt Sachs has a theory of cycles of musical styles each ascending, peaking, and then decaying within a time span of a century or so. Today, as someone has remarked, new style or at least a new technique or gimmick is conceived every twenty minutes. Whether or not that is so, it is impossible to include here every one of the latest developments in the choral styles of the twentieth century. A few examples of the important developments are discussed and used as exercises. Newer and other fashions should be explored further by both student and instructor.

AVE MARIA

From *Four Sacred Pieces*

Giuseppe Verdi

It may seem somewhat surprising to begin the section on aural problems with a work by Verdi, but the "Ave Maria" from the *Four Sacred Pieces* is quite a difficult piece to "tune" with a chorus; it is, therefore, an excellent composition on which to sharpen one's ear. The seven tone scale is an interesting one, and the harmony becomes very "restless" because it does not remain in one specific key for too long a period. Take a rather slow tempo ♩ = ca. 54 and wait until you are able to hear the harmony before you play it or sing it. Then play it at the piano to be sure you know the sound of each progression.

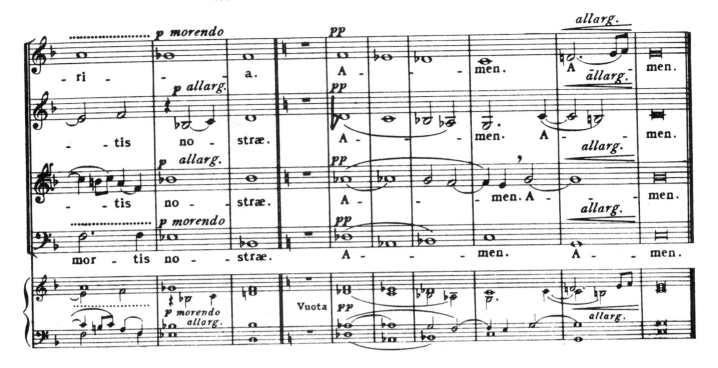

MIRABILE MYSTERIUM
Jacobus Gallus

Edited by Ferdinand Grossmann

In order to emphasize the thesis that a great many difficult aural problems exist in music written before this century, this unusual and moving work by the sixteenth-century composer Jacobus Gallus (also known as Jacob Handl) has been included. He was a contemporary of Carlo Gesualdo and, like the Italian composer, was extremely interested in giving complete expression to the mood of the text. He made considerable use of chromatic harmony and extremely abrupt changes of tonal centers, as is shown in this example. This kind of upsetting tonality creates pitch problems especially if the work is done a cappella. Special attention should be paid to the pitch when sudden cross-relations occur, and in the chromatic lines of the beginning, and again on page 4 of the score.

KYRIE
From *Mass in G Major*

Francis Poulenc

Francis Poulenc made a great contribution to choral music in the twentieth-century with many works both for a cappella chorus and for chorus with orchestral accompaniment. Here is a short excerpt from his *Mass in G Major,* which is for chorus a cappella. The excerpt was chosen because it is hard to "tune." The chords constantly skirt the regions of tension and release, and at 7 the intervals are sometimes difficult to negotiate cleanly. Special care must be taken in preparing the section between 9 and 10. It is suggested that the bass at first be separated from the rest of the choir, and added only after the other parts are rather secure. Though it should not be so, the rest just before 10 often rattles the chorus, and it is difficult to find the first chord at 10. A few practice sessions on that transition will give better results.

SIXTY-SEVENTH PSALM
Charles E. Ives

This is the first portion of *Psalm 67* by Charles Ives. It has been included here because the bitonality idea is clear and should be heard easily. The piece has wonderful sound but it is often done with too many pitch discrepancies as a result of squeamish conductors' ears. When presented with bitonality or polytonality make the chorus sing the dissonant notes with even more relish than the notes that fit conveniently into the "old-fashioned" harmonic scheme. A preliminary choral exercise for this work will be found at the end of the anthology. M.M. ♩ = 60.

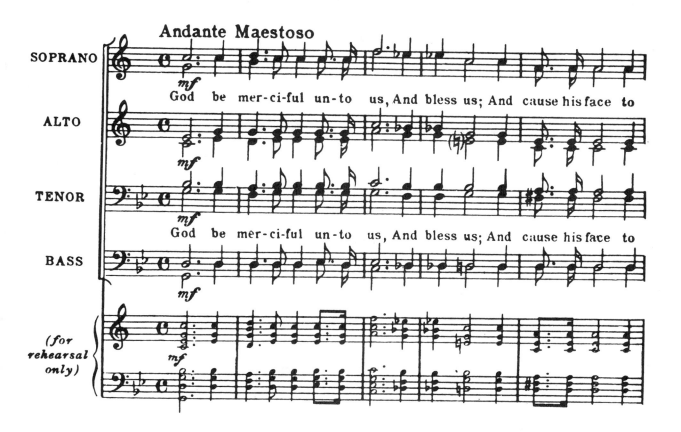

shine up-on us;   That thy way may be   known up-on earth, Thy sav-ing

shine up-on us;   That thy way may be   known up-on earth, Thy sav-ing

health a-mong all   na-tions. Let   the peo-ple   praise   thee, O

health a-mong all   na-tions. Let   the peo-ple   praise   thee, O

*This D is held if more than 8 voices

THERE WAS AN OLD MAN
From *Nonsense*

Music by Goffredo Petrassi

Words by Edward Lear

The second movement of Goffredo Petrassi's *Nonsense* cycle to words by Edward Lear is an example of what might be called mild choral pointillism. This means that different parts are given the next note in the line, i.e. if the line is C♭, F, A♭, D, G, G, F♯ the scheme is C♭-bass, F-tenor, A♭-alto, D-tenor, G-soprano, B-alto, F♯-soprano; all "points" add up to a single line. Petrassi, one of the leading contemporary Italian composers, writes not only the notes this way, but also the words. This is difficult to realize and perform, especially at a fast tempo; therefore, it is wise to make sure the joining of parts is smooth, and explain briefly to the chorus how this is to be done.

SARÀ DOLCE TACERE
Music by Luigi Nono

This excerpt from Luigi Nono's *Sarà Dolce Tacere* is an extreme case of choral pointillism. Seldom, if ever, does one voice have more than one note or a syllable before resting. The exact rhythmic portion of the beat at which a voice enters must be strongly felt by the conductor; it is urged that everyone feel the triplets, for this will facilitate the whole performance. The piece is for eight soloists and should be performed with the exact number. If the class is large, all the better. Pass the honors around, and make the others listen and criticize constructively. The meaning of the text is: "Also you are hills and paths of stone and play in bed of reeds, and you know the vineyard which in the night is silent."

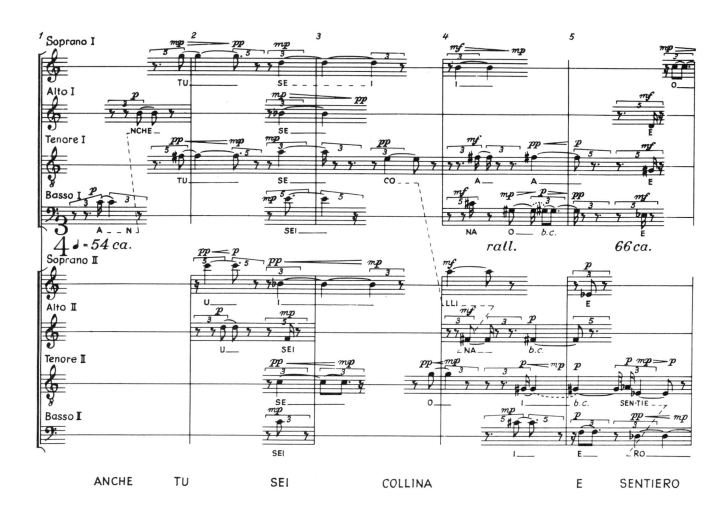

JOB

No. 6

Luigi Dallapiccola

An excerpt from the sacred drama *Job* by the dean of modern Italian composers, Luigi Dallapiccola. The work was written in 1950. While this portion is not strictly 12 tone, it is certainly non-tonal. Similarities in the lines (because of canonic devices) should help again in hearing the individual parts. Be sure that the chorus hears its first pitch from the accompaniment, and then finds its own way. The vocal lines, as in most of the work by this very lyrical composer, lend themselves to the voice and are beautiful to sing. The chorus dynamics are fortissimo throughout, but must be held back somewhat to execute a good crescendo and build a stirring ending. The text at this point reads: "And who confined with doors the sea, when breaking through He came out of the immense bosom."

CINQ RECHANTS, NO. 3
Olivier Messiaen

This is the first portion of the third movement of *Cinq Rechants* by Olivier Messiaen, who is generally acknowledged to be the father of such outstanding European avant-garde composers as Boulez and Stockhausen. Here is an example of his earlier writings, dating from 1948. Messiaen has been interested in music of India and of the Far East, and this is a piece which combines French words with Hindu-like words. The Hindu words are in Messiaen's own preface of an imaginary or pseudo-Hindu tongue. The tempo is quite slow; ♪ = 69 is suggested. The pitch is quite difficult to hear, but because of the orientation from static notes such as those found in the bass, it should be rather easy to overcome the difficulties. The French words mean: "My dress of love, my love, my prison of love made of light and air, my memory, my caress."

DU SOLLST NICHT, DU MUSST
From *Vier Stücke*

Arnold Schönberg

Here is an excerpt from the second of four pieces for mixed chorus, *Vier Stücke*, by Arnold Schönberg, dating from the year 1925. These are only available in this edition published with four different clefs (a very good exercise). In the Piano Suite, Opus 25 (1924), Schönberg utilized the 12-tone method in an entire work for the first time. After this innovation in these choruses, he seemed to deepen his interest in classical forms and contrapuntal practices. The first of this set of pieces is a double canon and is strictly carried through from beginning to end. The chorus quoted is a bit freer, but contains many fascinating contrapuntal devices, which should be carefully analyzed and used in the preparation of the piece. If approached contrapuntally, the work will be much easier to understand. (For the uninitiated four-clef readers, it should be stated that the first 5 notes have the same letter names.) The nonpoetic translation of the text is: "You shall not make yourself any kind of a picture (likeness). For a picture is limiting, it limits almost all that is limitless and should remain unrepresentative. A picture wants to have a name, but you could only name it something inconsequential, and that is not what you should treasure."

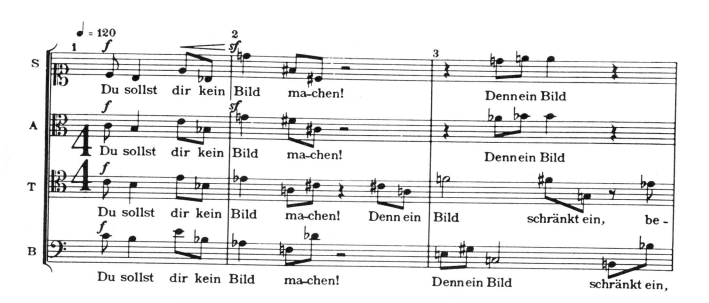

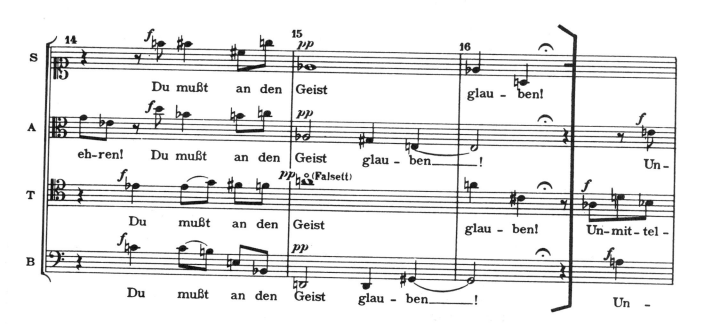

FIRST CANTATA
First Movement

Music by Anton Webern

Words by Hildegard Jone

English Version by Eric Smith

These are the first 9 measures of the first choral portion of Anton Webern's *First Cantata*, scored for soprano solo, mixed chorus and orchestra. The work was written in 1940. This is music written in the 12-tone technique, but whether you know the row or not does not matter. What counts is the spirit of the music and it is important that the difficult intervals, both vertical and horizontal, come out naturally and, of course, with clear and faultless intonation. Practice the intervals by twos and threes before putting them together. The conductor must have completely assimilated the sounds beforehand, and he will not take long to hear these. Tempo: the measures marked *getragen* (heavy or dragged) should be ♩ = 69 while the sections marked *lebhaft* (lively), should be taken at ♩ = 138. A preliminary choral exercise which will help with the preparation of this work can be found at the end of the anthology.

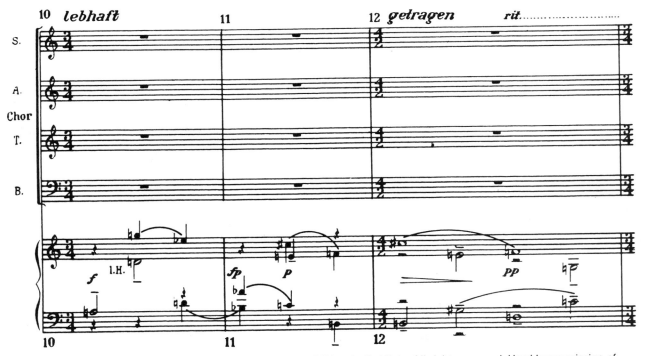

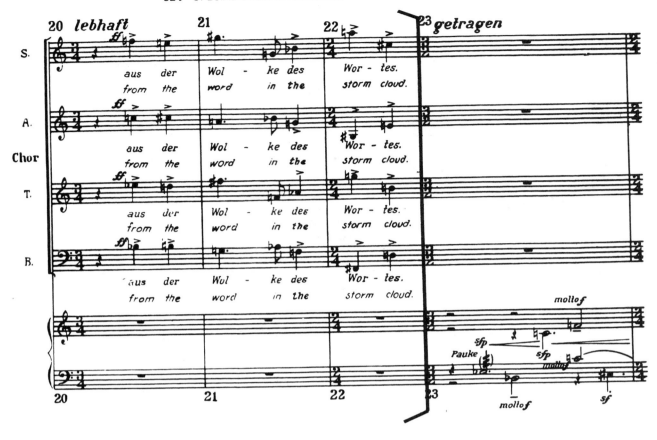

WORDS FROM WORDSWORTH

Nos. 1 & 2
Leon Kirchner

Leon Kirchner's *Words from Wordsworth* combines some speaking, in the manner of a *sprechstimme*, with music that often forms cluster sounds. It is important to learn how to hear these sounds. An exercise is suggested where four, five, then up to all 12 tones are sung close together. After doing this, take some of the sounds out of context and space them for all four voices; for instance take measure 8: have the altos double the basses and the sopranos double the tenors. Do the same for measure 12 and also transpose the basses (and altos) up an octave and listen to the close cluster sound. Then do the piece in tempo all the way through.

I

DE PROFUNDIS
Arnold Schönberg

The setting of Psalm 130 is Arnold Schönberg's last completed composition. It combines singing with rhythmically spoken passages. For this reason, it has been chosen to end the chapter on aural problems and to introduce Chapter 8 which will include quite a few speaking choir excerpts. Concerning the spoken parts the conductor should be particularly careful about pitch. This is not *sprechstimme*; it is rhythmically spoken material which should have mood, but only one pitch. The pianissimo places should be whispered, while the others should be spoken on one "pitch" designated either high, low or medium. "One pitch" means the same pitch for a passage, unless otherwise notated (on page 4). The difference between this treatment and *sprechstimme* is that the latter is "singsongy"; while this work is rather declamatory and should be much "drier" in sound. The voices marked ⊓ (meaning *hauptstimme* or principal voice) should be brought out. This "parentheses" is completed by an ending mark designated thus: ⌐ .

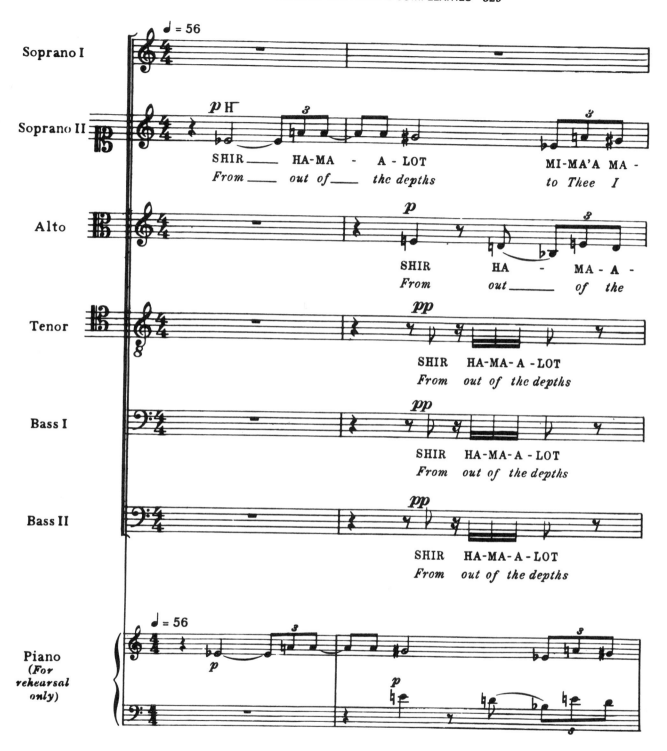

8
Contemporary Notation and the Speaking Chorus

Throughout the history of music, the composer has always been the innovator of new sounds and new techniques which have often caused great consternation and even hostility among audiences, performers, and fellow composers of a more conservative persuasion. The last quartets of Beethoven, the orchestration of Berlioz, and the harmonies of Wagner and Debussy, to mention only a few, were quite controversial subjects in their day. So, also, were the technical difficulties of the Brahms and Tschaikovsky violin concerti as well as the piano concerti by the same composers. Angry protestations are recorded in the accounts of the première of works by Stravinsky, Schönberg, Berg, and Webern. Time and history have taken care of these initial artistic judgments. Musicians have made peace with all these difficulties and have satisfactorily conquered such technical intricacies of the past as those in the Brahms and Tschaikovsky concerti which are now performed by most advanced students in our conservatories. And the once shocking works of the early twentieth century have long taken their place in the standard repertoire of our major organizations.

For many reasons toward some of which one may be sympathetic, the vocalist, the chorister, and also the choral conductor have been very slow in responding to the challenges of the contemporary composer. One may well be a bit sympathetic, for here we are dealing with the human instrument and not with anything manufactured. There are no valves, strings, or keys to help in the search for the pitch and, as seen in the previous chapter, many contemporary composers, especially those of the avant-garde, seem to have little or no regard for these limitations. Further, the composer of the fifties and sixties has greatly increased the demands upon the singer. In the early twentieth century occurred the emancipation of dissonance. This means that there is no longer such a phenomenon as a dissonant interval, but there are degrees of dissonance or simply greater and lesser degrees of tension. For instance, if a piece of music contains nothing but major sevenths, to end on a major second or a minor seventh would certainly be a relaxation of the tension according to the Hindemith tension scale which is based on the harmonic series.[1] Even popular music progressions are made up of successive seventh chords which many times fail to resolve in the "common practice" tradition and instead land on an idiomatic final jazz chord with the added sixth (c-e-g-a) giving us a second which remains unresolved at the very end.

Yet the last twenty years have seen a rapid development beyond this concern with tension and relaxation. Composers have now emancipated noise as a part of their musical language. Musique Concrete and purely electronic music have helped the composer to add many more sounds to his sonic palette which he has also tried to realize even when using existing nonelectronic forces. The extension of serialization not only of the notes but of all parameters such as rhythm, dynamics, timbre, tessitura and articulation has been paralleled by a trend toward less control of the individual's music, toward improvisation, aleatory, and chance music. Not only does this present tremendous vocal and aural problems for the singer, but composers have asked the singer to make sounds considered completely unvocal only a few years ago, and even to create his own music; a set of circumstances for which he has never been prepared. In addition to "Sprechstimme," all kinds of syllables and noises, body motions and actions have been incorporated into the vocabulary of choral music.

Our notational system has proven woefully inadequate for covering the multitude of sounds sought by our contemporary composers. No book has as yet been able to clarify or standardize the myriad symbols being employed for various effects. Hopefully, this will be accomplished soon for such projects are under way. Until we have agreed on systems of notation, however, we shall have to wade through instructional notes that are often more voluminous than the musical portion of the piece described.

With such a diversity of choral effects from which to choose, a few have been selected to aid the student in tackling similar works whenever he is confronted with them. Speaking chorus and occasional speaking effects are the most commonly used devices and, therefore, there are several of these. For the other works which have intricate notational problems, all the pertinent information which is supplied by the composer has been included. Read these carefully, and possibly work them out as a cooperative effort in class, but be sure to bring them to some kind of a satisfactory performance level, for notational problems, such as the ones quoted in this chapter, will become increasingly challenging.

[1] For a greater discussion of these points refer to *The Craft of Musical Composition*, Vol. I by Paul Hindemith, London: Schott and Co., 1937.

FUGUE IN DU

From *Well-Tempered Clavier*

J. S. Bach

Arranged by Bennett Williams

This chapter opens with two fun pieces, which contain no startling effects, but are rather novel all the same. During the past few years the Swingle Singers have had a great deal of success, and using these arrangements as encore pieces is a great deal of fun. There are no real problems for the conductor here except to keep a strong driving beat alive. Do not bother at all about the jazzy accompaniment, it will take care of itself, and will sound well only if the chorus sings the syllables straight and with rhythmic vitality. By all means use a drummer and a string bass.

HOLD ON
James Furman

There are many instances when we wish to perform authentic ethnic music, or "composed" music with an ethnic flavor. "Hold On," by James Furman, gives us an opportunity to look at a work that attempts to notate the Gospel singing style. James Furman is one of our foremost authorities on black Gospel music, and in this, as in some of his other works, he has given us as close an approximation as possible of all the rhythmic, melodic, and harmonic nuances of the style. The tempo is about ♩ = 112, and the composer begins the piece with the instruction "with driving force." Be sure that the syncopations are performed accurately while the beat remains very steady, and that the spirit of the performance "drives" jubilantly and exuberantly to the end. Begin the excerpt *mf* and build to a vivid and loud climax at the end.

PSALM 121
Heinz Werner Zimmerman

German composer Heinz Werner Zimmermann is widely known in this country for his choral music, especially those works that incorporate both instruments and techniques from jazz. He has, however, written many works that do not embody anything from the jazz genre, this being one lovely example. This unique setting of an often composed text presents the problem of coordinating an accompaniment of humming and whistling with sections that are sung normally. The technique of whistling is quite common today in both instrumental and choral works, and this piece gives a good opportunity for the class to practice its whistling prowess, while the conductor must listen carefully, since tuning a "whistling chorus" is a bit different from simply listening to a singing performance. Be sure to notice in the footnote that whistling always sounds an octave higher than notated. This excerpt should prove that a special effect such as whistling can create a beautiful, serene, almost celestial atmosphere.

*Whistling sounds one octave higher than notated.
**This reduction does not include the text bearing parts of this composition.

*Whistling sounds one octave higher than notated.

DEATH IS NOTHING TO US.

From *On the Nature of Things*

Music by Robert Starer

Words translated from Lucretius by James H. Mantinband.

Here is another very effective use of a singing and speaking chorus. This is the first of a group of choruses, *On the Nature of Things*, by Robert Starer. It should present no vocal or rhythmic problems, but it is quoted here to give the conductor an opportunity to practice teaching a group the smooth transition from singing to speaking, and then back again into singing. This may sound strange, but singers with no inhibitions about singing are almost embarrassed when they have to speak, and do so quite badly and without enough conviction or force to communicate.

weep and wail at death? If life is o-di-ous to you, why
_____ and wail? _____ If life is o-di-ous to you, why
dulge in all these lam-en - ta - tions? If life ___ is o-di-ous to you, why
ta - - tions? If life ___ is o-di-ous to you, why

GEOGRAPHICAL FUGUE
Ernst Toch

Surely this "Geographic Fugue" by Ernst Toch (1887–1964) is one of the classics among works for speaking chorus. This idiom is, of course, largely a creation of the twentieth century, probably an outgrowth of the newly generated interest in unpitched percussion instruments. A piece written solely for speaking chorus has a true kinship with works for unpitched percussion instruments. Therefore, the rhythm and the dynamics become the two major elements in presenting such a work successfully. Some composers have used nonsense syllables in such pieces, but Toch provides a geography lesson. Names of countries, towns, lakes, and rivers are the subjects of the rhythmic feast. The task of the conductor is to choose a tempo that will allow the chorus to articulate each word clearly, basing the choice of tempo on the expectation that the notation becomes faster with the sixteenth note triplet eventually forming the fastest rhythm. To perform this piece with the greatest success, the chorus must learn to care especially about its pronunciation of consonants, and of course practice the "tongue twisters" until they become second nature.

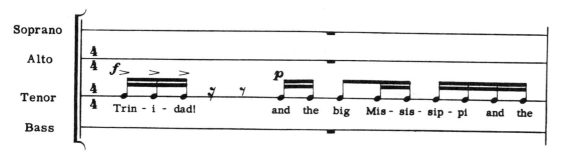

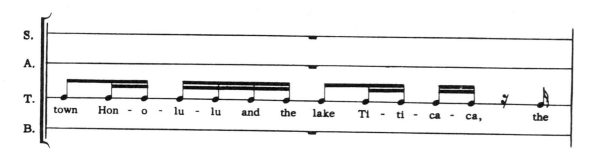

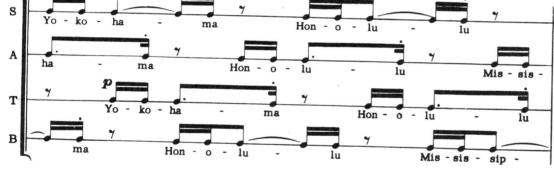

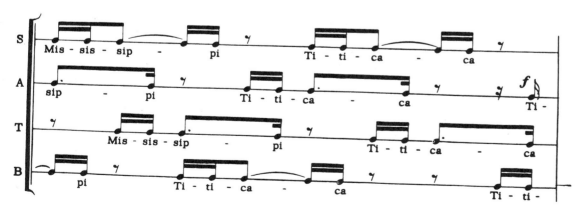

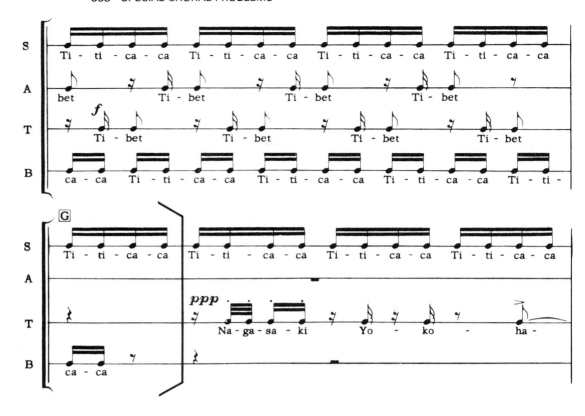

CHANGES

Part I

Gordon Crosse

Gordon Crosse, one of England's prominent young composers, is represented here with a simple improvisation from his "nocturnal cycle," *Changes*, for soprano and baritone, mixed chorus, and orchestra. It is necessary to provide an arythmic background, first for the soprano soloist, and then for the orchestra. The tempo is allegromolto or ♩ = 96–100. The chorus should be brought in and then allowed to repeat their part ad libitum during the singing of the solo part, the playing of the orchestra part at D, and through the rest. Bring in the orchestra (one measure after C) only when the background has been established to your satisfaction. It will take more than two beats; however the cutoff must be uniform and come before 17 no matter on what notes the chorus happens to land.

SICUT LOCUTUS EST
From *Magnificat*

Alan Hovhaness

Here is another, slightly different, example of a choral cadenza or improvised passage. The conductor's job is quite simple in this excerpt from Alan Hovhaness' *Magnificat.* The composer creates a kind of musical curtain. The conductor gives a downbeat and the chorus repeats the assigned parts at will but, as the composer states, "not together." Be sure that the passage does not last too long, and build the curtain of sound from a pianissimo to a triple forte, then let it almost decay before the cutoff.

LO, HOW A ROSE E'ER BLOOMING
Hugo Distler

English text adapted by Karl Lishinsky

Distler was one of the most prolific choral composers of the early part of our century. Besides many original choral works, he also devoted much of his great talent to choral arrangements of preexisting themes. His style was greatly influenced by Medieval and Renaissance music, and many of his pieces present problems to the conductor because of Distler's insistence on placing the bar lines for each part according to the structure of the accents. The result is a strange-looking score in which the bar lines seem to be a hindrance rather than an aid. However, when one performs each voice part separately, comprehension of the composer's logic becomes quite easy. It is suggested that the conductor use a $\frac{4}{4}$ pattern throughout, emphasizing the downbeats only on those measures where all voices coincide (measures 1, 6, 7, 8, etc.). Because of this notation and the resultant rhythmic intricacy, the conductor must try diligently to give all the entrances to the voices that do not come in at the beginning of each verse.

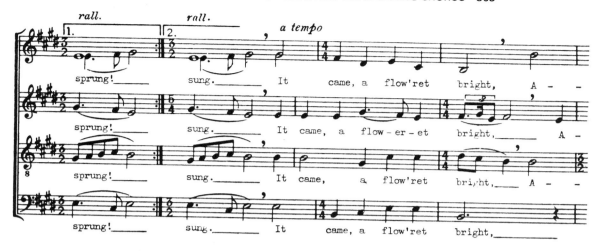

INTRODUCTION

From *Moon Canticle*

Music by Leslie Bassett

Words from Paradise Lost
by John Milton

Here is an excerpt from a work written in the summer of 1969 by Leslie Bassett called *Moon Canticle*. It has a solo cello, a narrator, and a large mixed chorus. If there is no cello available, piano accompaniment should be used. Even though, as the composer states, no definite pitches are necessary, the "sh" and "ping" parts should be assigned, in order to approximate the level of pitch and then, as is stated in the note (below the music), the "Ah" blocks should start off on the assigned pitch levels. The tempo is ♩ = 69. Do not try to synchronize either the "sh" or "ping" sounds, but let the singers determine when they are to come in by a kind of proportional notation; that is, let them judge where in the two beats their sound fits. The "Ah" 's should be in time. At W the sound band means "a texture formed by multiple articulations of the words or sounds underlaid." It is not necessary for the singers to be together, and no particular pitch is dictated.

At "Ping" the sections are divided into 4 or 5 groups. Singers in each group enter independently at random pitch and order, sustaining their notes until "Ah." "Ah" opens with the pitches established during "Ping."

PSALM 77
Knut Nystedt

The Scandinavian composer Knut Nystedt became popular in America during the 1960s and 1970s for his choral pieces using special effects such as speaking, shouting, moaning, tongue-clicking, and other devices combined with rather simple, straightforward music. Here is an example of such a piece, which contains some of these effects easily notated for instant comprehension. One measure after A the basses, followed in turn by the other voices, are asked to "moan" quietly and at a certain "pitch level." At the seventh measure after A all voices are asked to perform a *glissando* to their very lowest pitches. The triangle pointing downward is the accepted symbol of the lowest possible pitch. For greatest effectiveness of this passage, it should be executed strictly in rhythm so as not to oversentimentalize the effect. The spoken passage thereafter should be performed at a low whisper. The rest of this piece is notated in conventional notation except for two pages in the middle, which are also quoted here. The composer is quite specific as to "pitch height," but the conductor should use his sense of judgment as to what is meant by high, medium, and low "speaking levels." Of course the required dynamics must be carefully observed throughout.

Excerpt 1:

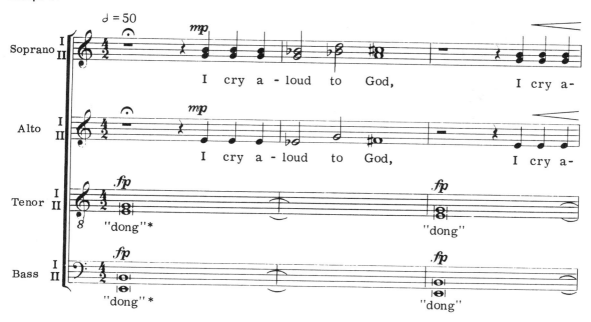

* Go to the "ng" immediately.
2. Bass: "daw"

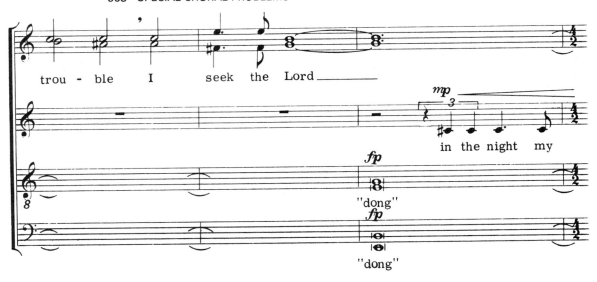

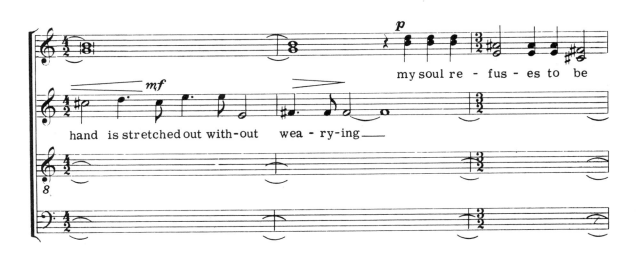

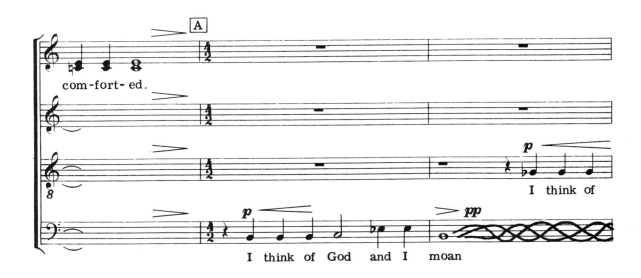

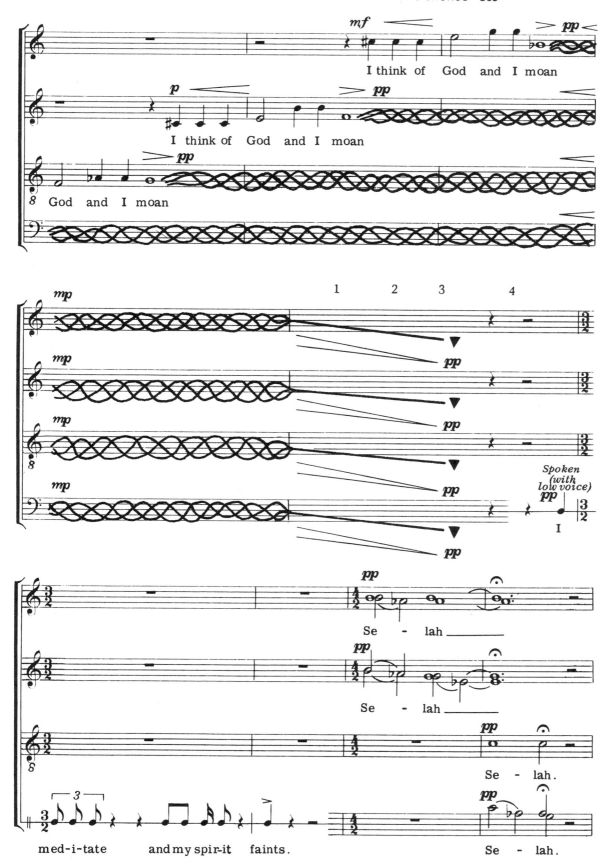

Excerpt 2:

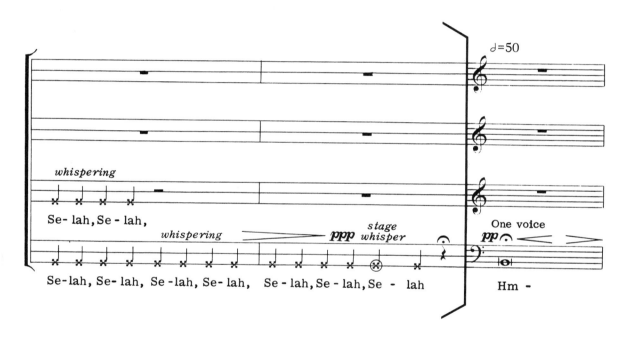

ALLELUIA
Daniel Pinkham

Daniel Pinkham is one of America's most prolific choral composers. He has written both a cappella and accompanied music, and his cantatas for Christmas and Easter have become special favorites in our choral repertoire. This is an excerpt from a different Easter Set that employs tape as the accompanying "instrument." Though the tape does not accompany the excerpt, it was felt that the exercise of performing a small portion of this piece was important enough and could be accomplished effectively even without the tape. Some sustaining instrument should be used to give an "A" drone whenever the tape is indicated. Since there is as yet no standard notation for many of the choral effects for which Pinkham calls, it is imperative that the conductor read the instructions carefully and understand the notation. Before the entire excerpt is attempted, the conductor should explain the notation to the choir and practice each effect separately. It is helpful to use a stopwatch as the composer suggests, even though the tape is not available for this exercise. Of course, if this piece is to be performed, the tape can be obtained from the publisher.

TAPE — The tape is 7 1/2 ips. quarter-track stereo, available for sale from the publisher. Once started it runs for the duration of the work. The tape level should be set to balance the chorus and should be heard clearly at all times except when the chorus is singing *fortissimo*.

THE ANTIPHONAL VOICES — Three or more women singers should be placed in various parts of the auditorium. Their parts should not be synchronized and they should strive to maintain individuality of tempo and mood. Each should be able easily to see the conductor and the other soloists. At the appropriate places the conductor will point to any one of them, who immediately begins to sing any one of the melodic phrases and completes it. At the point where the asterisk (*) appears in her phrase she signals to another soloist to start a contrasting or complementary phrase. This singer, when reaching the asterisk in her turn, signals yet another singer to enter. At a sign from the conductor whatever woman is singing completes her phrase and then stops.

PRONUNCIATION — As if spelled *ah-leh-loo-yah* in English.

ACCIDENTALS — Accidentals continue in effect until cancelled.

STOPWATCH — A stopwatch or other timing device is essential. Start the stopwatch at the entrance of the first tape sound.

NOTATION

Gradually one by one members of a section enter until all are singing. Singers should choose the lowest possible pitch on which they can make a resonant sound.

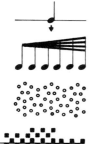

A single low note of indeterminate pitch. Each singer chooses the lowest resonant note in his register.

A gradual accelerando which keeps the same dynamic level throughout.

A texture made up of speaking and singing in a medium register, using random pitches and speeds.

A tone cluster whose high or low pitch is indicated by the position in relation to the median line. When the cluster moves, all notes are connected by a glissando. All notes are to be sung.

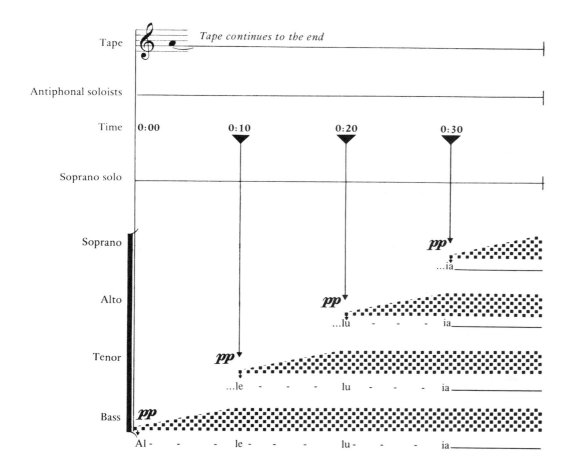

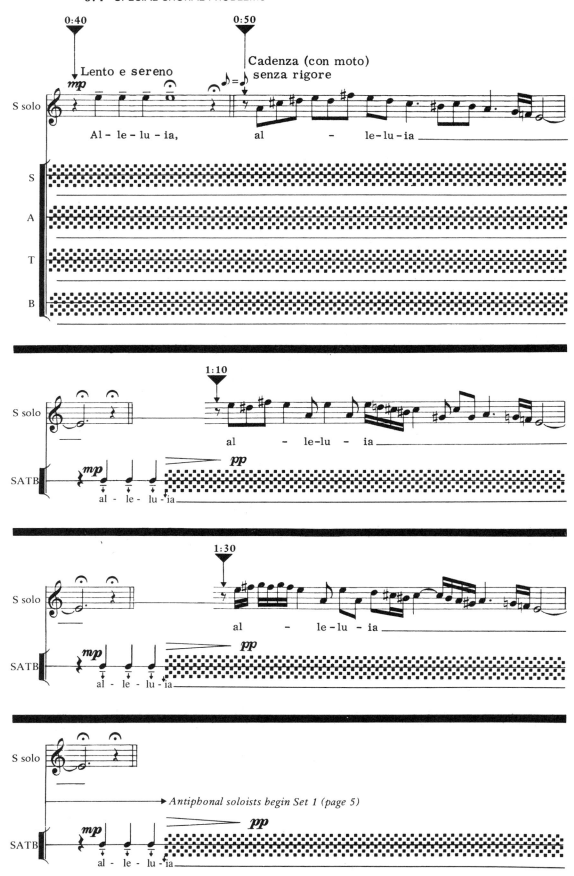

Antiphonal soloists begin Set 1 (page 5)

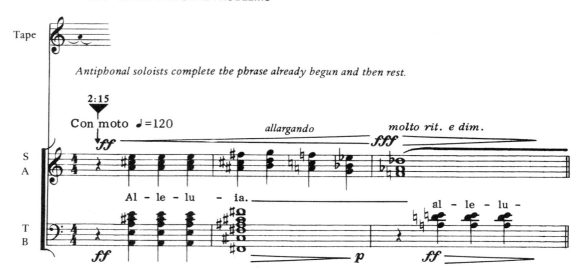

Antiphonal soloists complete the phrase already begun and then rest.

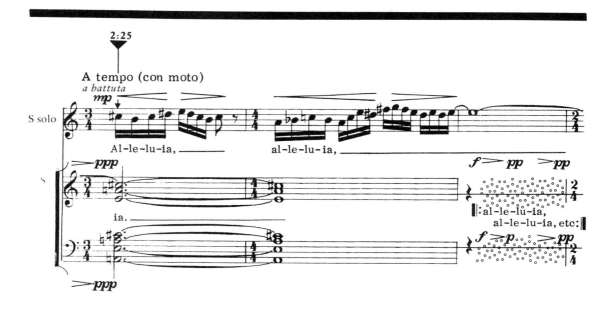

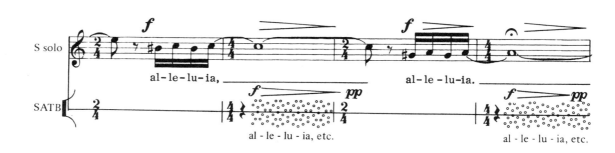

STABAT MATER

From *St. Luke Passion*

Krzysztof Penderecki

The "Stabat Mater" is a portion of the *St. Luke Passion,* the first of the highly successful choral works written by Penderecki. This portion of the *Passion* may be performed separately, for it is the only section that is a cappella. All kinds of effects are demanded, and the conductor should consult the guide to the notation and practice each of the special requirements separately before putting the entire piece together. This is a work of great beauty, religiosity, and originality, and every effort must be made to bridge the difficulties in the score, so that its beauty and effectiveness not be marred by any kind of seeming strain in the performance of the music.

Guide to the Notation

♩ = falsetto

♩ = like a recitative (in other words, "spoken")

♩ = murmuring

MUSIC FOR THE ASCENSION
Elliott Schwartz

The most important task facing the conductor before attempting this piece is to read and completely absorb the instructions preceding the music. It is a semi-aleatoric work. Why "semi"? Because the indeterminacy factor has very little to do with supplying pitches or free improvisation, but instead provides for the construction of certain phrases at the conductor's discretion, giving the conductor some freedom as to the exact places of entry of the chorus vis-à-vis the accompaniment. The instructions are quite clear, and should answer all questions concerning the composer's intention as well as his notation. Pieces of this type exist today in great profusion, and it is important for any conductor to be able to manage them with ease. This will convey a sense of seriousness of purpose to the chorus and assure a most satisfactory performance.

INSTRUCTIONS

CHORUS

One person in each of the four "sections" (S. A. T. and B.) is to play a percussion instrument, as follows:

S.   Suspended cymbal
A.
T. } 3 tenor drums or "tom toms" - in descending pitch, (A) (T) (B)
B.   i. e. each person has one drum.

Hard- and soft-headed drumsticks are needed in each of these four solo percussion parts: 2 sticks (1 hard, 1 soft) for the cymbal; 4 sticks (2 hard, 2 soft) for each of the drummers.

NOTATION

Almost all choral setting here is syllabic. The lone exception occurs on page 11 where pitches extending in melisma over a syllable are joined by a dotted slur: ⌒

⌒ = tone goes notably flat or sharp, i. e. "slide" or "gliss".

Improvise on these pitches for two beats = For the duration specified and at specified dynamics, sing the
pp pitches in any order, rhythm, repeating any number of times - moderate to rapid motion. Begin preferably with first pitch in the box.

♩ outside each of the four staves (S. A. T. and B.) = percussion. *H. S.* = hard stick(s)
✗ *S. S.* = soft stick(s)

In a number of instances the chorus is to function independently of the other elements (organ, narrator), i.e. sing two short passages at some time of your choosing, within a given duration ("8 beats"). These will be cued by the conductor, with the exception of the passages for solo voices on page 5 and page 12. In all such cases, do not attempt to coordinate or synchronize with other elements (except other voices, and not even then in the solo passages).

NARRATOR

He is to be situated at a distance from the chorus, preferably at a side wall or rear wall. On cue he is to read a selection from the Epistle for Ascension day (Acts I: 7,8,9,10,11), subdivided into two parts.

1 "And he said unto them, it is not for you to know the times or the seasons" - - - (ending with) "and a cloud received him out of their sight." 1 minute (Acts I: 7,8,9)
2 "And while they looked steadfastly towards heaven" - - - (ending with) "shall so come in like manner as ye have seen him go into heaven." 30 seconds (Acts I: 10,11)

Read slowly and deliberately as though the chorus and organ were not present. Do NOT attempt to synchronize or coordinate with them.

ORGAN

Manuals only, no pedal. The manuals should be contrasted so that [A] in the score refers to a dry, crisp, woodwind timbre, extreme registers outlined. Use no 8's, only 16', 4' and 2'; or 16' and 4'; or 16' and 2'. [B] should refer to a more resonant combination of 8's, trumpet, viola, etc. No 16' or 2', perhaps 4' at the discretion of the performer.

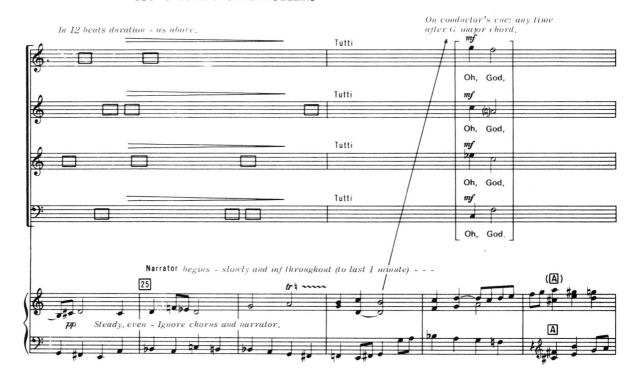

APPENDIXES

Exercises
to Introduce the Chorus
to Difficult Passages

Introductory "warming-up" exercises for:

IN THE BEGINNING
Aaron Copland

1. During the course of the "warming-up" explain *pandiatonicism* and *pantonality.*
2. Sing these two exercises in unison, then as a 2-, 3-, and 4-voice canon repeating each three times (on "ah" and "ooh").

You may begin on any pitch.

3. Sing in unison starting on various pitches and on different syllables.

4. Cadences.

5. Clap these rhythms, accenting sharply.

6. Sing on "tah" or "doo."

7. Tenors and altos hold the "B," while sopranos sing top, and basses bottom line.

a.

b. Build a "fan" (may be started on any pitch).

Introductory "warming-up" exercises for:

SIXTY-SEVENTH PSALM
Charles Ives

1. During the course of the warming-up explain *duotonality* and *polytonality*.
2. Sing
   a. On "loh." b. On "tah."

   c. On "la."

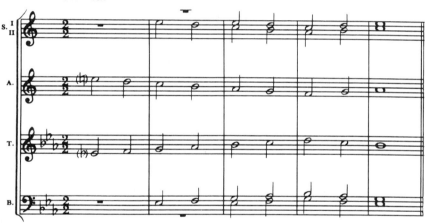

   d. On "doo."

Introductory "warming-up" exercises for:

KANTATE I
Anton Webern

1. During the course of the warming-up, explain briefly the principles of *nontonality*, *12-tone techniques*, and *serialization.*
2. Sing this row in unison on "la." Then sing it backward (retrograde).

3. Sing in 3 parts (3 note "cell" from "P").

Transpose to several starting pitches.

4. Sing in 4 parts (chords from the beginning of the work utilizing the "R" and "I" permutation).

5. Sing "P"rime against "I"nversion.

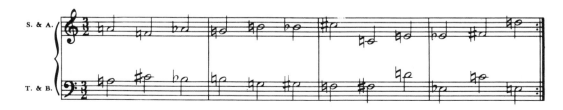

6. Sing this canon (women P⁷, men I⁹); repeat 3 times.

7. Sing slowly in 4 parts on a bright syllable.

Pronunciation Guide

LATIN	ITALIAN	FRENCH	GERMAN
Vowels	**Vowels**	**Vowels**	**Vowels**
a = father	a = father	a = father	a = pun (Antwort)
e = red	e (open) = met	à = rat	a = father (Vahr)
i = see	e (closed) = rate	au = bow	ä = no English equilavent but International Phonetics (ae) or (e:)
o = swarm	i = see	autr = knot	e = head
u = spoon	o = swarm	e, è = record (père)	i = bit or be
ae = say	u = spoon	e, é = day (été)	o = not or note
oe = say		e = earth (je)	u = foot or boot
	Consonants	eu = no English equivalent (Dieu) German "ö"	ü = No English equivalent International Phonetics (y)
Consonants	b = b	i = piece	ö = similar to the above I.P.A. (o)
b = b	c = ch before i and e; k before h, a, o, u	o = ought	
c = change before e, i, ae, oe; otherwise c = k	d = d	oi = swat	**Diphthongs**
d = d	f = f	u = no English equivalent (tu) German "ü"	ei, ai = my
f = f	g = soft before i and e; hard before h, a, o, u	**Nasal Vowels**	au = house
g = soft before e, i, ae, oe; hard otherwise	h = used only to harden c, g, s, c, otherwise silent	When a vowel is followed in the same syllable by m or n the vowel is nasalized and the m or n not pronounced.	eu, au = coy
h = either like k between letters "nihil" otherwise silent	l = l	quand is like Kaun	ui = Louis
j = y	m = m	tempt is like taump	
k = k	n = n	cinq is like sank	**Consonants**
l = l	p = p	bon is like "bonbon"	b = b except at the end of a word it becomes almost p
m = m	q = k	un = munch	c = k
n = n	r = r but must be rolled		ch = k at the beginning of a word. After a, o, u, au it becomes (x) like Bach (guttural). After e, i, o, u, eu it becomes soft like the English word beige
gn = ny (agnus)	s = z between two vowels or before two voiced consonant; otherwise "s"	**Consonants**	
p = p	t = t	b = b, but silent when final	
ph = f	v = v	c = k at the end of a word and before a, o, u, l and r	
q = k	x = ks	ç = s	(ch) = the combination chs becomes x or ks
r = r (slightly rolled)	z = dz or ts	cc = k	d = d at the beginning of a syllable but hardens to t at the end of a syllable
s = s	gl = lli as in billion	ch = k	
t = t	gn = ny as in canyon	ch = sh	
v = v	sc = sh before i and e, sk before h, a, o, u		
x = x			
z = dz			

RUSSIAN

Since both Russian and Hebrew have their own alphabet, this list will only reflect the symbols used in the transliteration for use in English-speaking countries.

Vowels

a = father
è = let
e = date
i = meet
o = oral
u = spoon
y = sin
ye = yes
ya = yard

Consonants

z = zone
ch = change
sh = shall
kh = the guttural ch as in the name Bach

HEBREW

a = father
e = red
i = see
o = oral
u = spoon
e = day

Consonants

ch = guttural (Bach)
g = go
h = hope
r = r (slightly rolled)
s = sun
sh = shall
y = yes
z = zoo

An apostrophe after a consonant (y', v', p') is pronounced like a neutral vowel as in the first syllable of the word "variety." Where a syllabic value is not indicated musically the apostrophe is to be ignored

---

d = d except when linked to a word beginning with a vowel it becomes t; quand-il
f = f
g = g before a, ou, l or r; zj before e, i, y
gn = nyuh
gu = g
h = always silent
j = zj
k = k
l = l but y when preceded by "ai" or "ei"
ll = yuh
m = m except if it is nasalized
mm = m
n = n except when it is nasalized
nn = n
q = k
qu = k
r = r (slightly rolled); silent in "er" endings
s = s except z between vowels z when linked, silent when final.
sc = sk before a, o, u, l and r
ss = s
t = t
ti = s in "tion" endings
v = v
x = ks and "z" when linked, silent when final
y = y
z = z, silent in verb ending (ez)

---

dt = t
f = f
g = g but at the end of a syllable after a, e, o, u it becomes k; and at the end of a syllable after i, it becomes soft like in beige
h = h but silent after vowels and after t
j = y in the word year
k = k
l = l
m = m
n = n
ng = ng (sing)
nk = nk (bank)
p = p
ph = f
qu = kv
r = r not always rolled
s = z at the beginning of a syllable, but just like the English "s" at the end of one
ss = s
sch = sh (shoe)
sp = shp at the beginning of a word, but as in English elsewhere
st = sht
t = t
v = f
w = v
x = ks
z = ts

SPANISH

Vowels

a = father
e = met (neither too open nor too closed)
i = see
o = warm (neither too open nor too closed)
u = spoon

Consonants

b = b as an initial consonant or after m or n it becomes "v" as all other interior sounds "giboso" is pronounced "givosoh"
c = c except before e or i when it becomes "th"
ch = ch as in church
d = d as an initial consonant or after "l" and "n"; otherwise it is pronounced like a "th"
f = f
g = g but before "e" or "i" always as English "h"
h = silent
j = like English "h"
k = k
l = l
ll = y
m = m
n = n except before b, f, m, p and v when it becomes "m"
ñ = ny
p = p
q = q is used before silent "u" to form the sound of "k"
r = r before a vowel with one flip of the tongue; when it is the final letter it is trilled lightly, and when doubled it is trilled heavily
s = s except before voiced consonants whether in the same word or the next and before words beginning with the sound of "w" or "y," "s" is pronounced like the English "z"
t = t
v = v
x = "ks" between two vowels or "s" before another consonant
y = same as letter "i" meet; in combination with "o" it becomes "boy"
z = like z in haze except before any voiced consonants (b, d, l, g, etc.) it becomes "th"

List of the Publishers
and Their Works

Alexander Broude Music Publishers, Inc., 1619 Broadway, New York, N.Y. 10019
"Wave All the Flags in the Country" by G. P. Telemann, pp. 3–5
Associated Music Publishers, 605 Fifth Avenue, New York, N.Y. 10020
"Psalm" from *Psalm and Prayer* by Walter Piston, pp. 7–8.
"Psalm 123" by Norman Lockwood, pp. 1–3
"Psalm 67" by Charles Ives, pp. 1–2
"Words from Wordsworth" (Nos. 1 and 2), by Leon Kirchner, pp. 3–6
Baerenreiter-Verlag, Kassel, West Germany
"Lo, How a Rose E'er Blooming" by Hugo Distler, pp. 2–3
Belmont Music, 116 Rockingham Avenue, Los Angeles, California 90049
"Du sollst nicht, du musst" from "Vier Stücke," Opus 27, No. 2, by Arnold
Schönberg, pp. 9–10
Belwin-Mills Music Publishers (Colombo-Ricordi), 1790 Broadway, New York, N.Y.
10019
"Stan' Still Jordan" by Fela Sowande, pp. 2–5
"Sixth Madrigal" from "The Unicorn" by Gian Carlo Menotti, pp. 74–77
Belwin-Mills Music Publishers (Mills Music)
"Geographical Fugue" by Ernst Toch, pp. 1–6
Belwin-Mills Music Publishers (Salabert)
"Domine Fili" from *Gloria* by Francis Poulenc, pp. 28–33
"Cinq Rechants" (No. 3), by Oliver Messiaen, pp. 15–16

Belwin-Mills Music Publishers (Schott)
    "Kryie" from *Messe* by Paul Hindemith, pp. 1–2
    "Since All is Passing" from *Six Chansons* by Paul Hindemith, p. 2
    "A Swan" from *Six Chansons"* by Paul Hindemith, pp. 2–3
    "Uf dem anger" from *Carmina Burana* by Carl Orff, pp. 26–27 (vocal score),
        pp. 43–46 (orchestral score)
Boosey & Hawkes, 30 West 57th Street, New York, N.Y. 10019
    "Dies Irae" from "War Requiem" by Benjamin Britten, pp. 59–62
    "Festival Te Deum" by Benjamin Britten, pp. 2–5
    "Veni Sancte Spiritus" by Peter Maxwell Davies, pp. 7–8
    "Omnes Gentes" by Gordon Binkerd, pp. 2–3
    "Autumn Flowers" by Gordon Binkerd, pp. 1–2
    "On Visiting Oxford" from *A Nation of Cowslips* by Dominick Argento, pp. 2–5
    "Make We Joye Nowe in This Fest" from *A Christmas Offering* by Gail Kubik,
        pp. 10–11
    "Walking on the Green Grass" by Michael Hennagin, pp. 2–4
    "God, Bring Thy Sword" by Ron Nelson, pp. 3–5
    "Russian Credo" by Igor Stravinsky, pp. 3–6
    "Symphony of Psalms" by Igor Stravinsky, p. 13 (vocal score), pp. 1–6
        (orchestral score)
    "Gloria" from *Mass* by Igor Stravinsky, pp. 7–8
    "Wainamoinen Makes Music" by Zoltán Kodály, pp. 7–8
    "In the Beginning" by Aaron Copland, pp. 17–23
    "Laudate Dominum" (No. 1) from *Cinque Laude* by Norman Dinerstein, p. 2
    "An Egg" from *Homer's Woe* by Jack Beeson, p. 10
    "Greener Pastures" by Jack Beeson, pp. 2–4
Broude Brothers, 56 West 45th Street, New York, N.Y. 10036
    "O Come Let Us Sing" by Jean Berger, pp. 2–4
    "Adonoy Yimloch" from *Sacred Service* by Ernst Bloch, pp. 18–20
Concordia Publishing House, 3558 South Jefferson Avenue, St. Louis, Missouri
63118
    "Kyrie" from *Missa de Angelis* by Robert Crane, pp. 3–4
European American Music, P.O. Box 850, Valley Forge, Pennsylvania 19482
    "Morning" by György Ligeti (B. Schott's Soehne), pp. 6–9
    "Sara Dolce Tacere" by Luigi Nono (Ars Viva Verlag)
    First Cantata (First Movement) (Universal Edition) by Anton Webern, pp. 2–3
Carl Fischer, Inc., 56–62 Cooper Square, New York, N.Y. 10003
    "Three Descants" (No. 1), from *Ecclesiastes* by Karl Kohn, pp. 3–5
    "Cherubic Hymn" by Howard Hanson, pp. 18–19
    "Psalm 51" from *Pilgrim Psalms* by Ross Lee Finney, pp. 48–49
    "Caligaverunt Oculi Mei" by Tomás Luis de Victoria, pp. 2–4
    "Psalms" by Lukas Foss, pp. 26–31
    "Bless Ye the Lord" by M. Ippolitov-Ivanov (Wilhousky), pp. 4–6
    "Psalm 121" by Heinz Werner Zimmerman, pp. 2–5
    "Music for the Ascension" by Elliott Schwartz, pp. 2–7
Galaxy Music Corporation, 2121 Broadway, New York, N.Y. 10023
    Rounds in $\frac{6}{8}$, $\frac{3}{4}$, and $\frac{4}{4}$ Time
    "Psalm 148" by Gustav Holst, pp. 1–3
    "April Is in My Mistress' Face" by Thomas Morley, pp. 6–8
    "Kyrie Eleison" from *Mass for Four Voices* by William Byrd, pp. 2–3
    "Give Thanks Unto the Lord" by Robert Starer, pp. 1–2
    "O Clap Your Hands" by Ralph Vaughan Williams, pp. 8–12
Lawson-Gould Music Publishers, Inc., 609 Fifth Avenue, New York, N.Y. 10017
    "Jack der Spratt" from *Songs Mein Grossmama Sang* by Lloyd Pfautsch,
        pp. 6–7

"Gloria" from "Misa Criolla" by Ariel Ramirez, pp. 10–12

"Liebeslieder Walzer" Opus 52, No. 8, by Johannes Brahms, pp. 22–23

E. B. Marks Music Corporation, 136 West 52nd Street, New York, N.Y. 10019

"Kyrie" from *Missa Iste Confessor* by Giovanni Palestrina, pp. 5–9

"You Have Ravished My Heart" by Stephen Chatman, pp. 3–6

"Ave Maria" by Anton Bruckner, pp. 3–6

M. C. A. Music, 445 Park Avenue, New York, N.Y. 10022

"The Lamb" from *The Wondrous Kingdom* by Mark Bucci, pp. 6–8

"There Was an Old Man" from *Nonsense* by Goffredo Petrassi, pp. 10–12

"Death Is Nothing to Us" from *On the Nature of Things* by Robert Starer, pp. 3–5

M. C. A. Music (Israeli Music Publishers)

"I Will Life Up Mine Eyes" by Paul Ben-Haim, p. 3

"De Profundis" by Arnold Schönberg, pp. 2–7

M. C. A. Music (Zerboni)

"Job" (No. 6), by Luigi Dallapiccola, pp. 59–61

Merion Music, Bryn Mawr, Pennsylvania 19010

"Coventry Carol" by Sidney Hodkinson, pp. 2–5

Music 70, 170 N.E. 33rd St., Fort Lauderdale, Florida 33334

"Hold On" by James Furman, pp. 8–11

Oxford University Press, 200 Madison Avenue, New York, N.Y. 10016

"The Cricket" by Josquin des Prés, pp. 1–2

"Magnificat" from *Second Service* by Thomas Thomkins, pp. 1–3

"Awake! Do Not Cast Us Off" by Samuel Adler, pp. 4–5

"Changes" (Part 1) by Gordon Crosse, pp. 9–10

"Kyrie Eleison" from *Mass in C* by John Gardner, pp. 2–3

"Belshazzar's Feast" by William Walton, pp. 55–59

C. F. Peters Corporation, 373 Park Avenue South, New York, N.Y. 10016

"Introduction" from *Moon Canticle* by Leslie Bassett, p. 3

"Sicut Locutus Est" from *Magnificat* by Alan Hovhaness, p. 37

"Glory to God" by Alan Hovhaness, pp. 15–18

"By the Rivers of Babylon" by David Amram, pp. 9–11

"Psalm 112" (No. 8) by G. F. Handel, pp. 38–43

"A Lincoln Letter" by Ulysses Kay, pp. 12–15

Pride (permission granted by the composer for the publisher), Mr. Nicholas Flagello, 120 Montgomery Circle, New Rochelle, N.Y. 10804

"Virtue" by Nicolas Flagello, pp. 2–4

Samuel Fox Publishing Company, 1841 Broadway, New York, N.Y. 10023

"Fugue in Du" Arranged by Bennett Williams from *Well-Tempered Clavier* by J.S. Bach, pp. 3–6

E. C. Schirmer, 221 Columbus Avenue, Boston, Massachusetts 02116

"Say Ye to the Righteous" from *The Peaceable Kingdom* by Randall Thompson, pp. 13–14

"Lark" by Aaron Copland, p. 12.

"If That the Peace of God" by Warren Benson, pp. 3–4

Psalm: "All Praise to Him" from *King David* by Arthur Honegger, p. 7

"Alleluia" by Daniel Pinkham, pp. 2–6

G. Schirmer, Inc., 609 Fifth Avenue, New York, N.Y. 10017

"Alleluia, Haec Dies" by Ignazio Donati, pp. 3–5 (Faber)

"Holiday Song" by William Schuman, pp. 5–6

"Behold, My Saviour Now Is Taken" from *St. Matthew Passion,* by J. S. Bach, pp. 80–83.

"A Jubilant Song" by Norman Dello Joio, pp. 2–3, 20–23

"Alleluia" from "Brazilian Psalm" by Jean Berger, pp. 2–5

"Kaddish, Symphony No. 3" by Leonard Bernstein

"Chichester Psalms" (No. 3) by Leonard Bernstein, pp. 37–39
"Inscription" from *Symphony for Voices* by Roy Harris, pp. 5–7
"God's Time Is the Best" from *Cantata No. 106* by J. S. Bach, pp. 2–5
"I Never Saw a Moor" by Robert Muczynski, pp. 2–3
"Lament" from "The Hour-Glass" by Irving Fine, pp. 3–5
"The Death of the Bishop of Brindisi" by Gian Carlo Menotti, pp. 33–37
"Spring Song" from *The Lark* by Leonard Bernstein, pp. 12–14
"Prayers of Kierkegaard" by Samuel Barber, pp. 13–15
"Cantate Domino" by Heinrich Schütz, pp. 2–7
"Mirabile Mysterium" by Jacobus Gallus, pp. 1–6
"Benedictus" from *Mass in G minor* by Ralph Vaughan Williams, pp. 38–41
"Kyrie" from *Mass in G Major* by Francis Poulenc, pp. 4–6
Schmitt Hall & McCreary Company, Minneapolis, Minnesota
"Fire, Fire, My Heart" by Thomas Morley, pp. 1–5
Shawnee Press, Delaware Water Gap, Pennsylvania 18327
"Set Down Servant" arranged by Robert Shaw, pp. 4–8
Southern Music Publishing Co., Inc., 1619 Broadway, New York, N.Y. 10019
"Chorale" by David Diamond, pp. 3–4
"Until Day and Night Shall Cease" from *Hebrew Cantata* by Harold Shapero, pp. 70–73
"In Certainty of Song" by Wallingford Riegger, pp. 16–17
"To Music" by Elliott Carter, pp. 8–10
Theodore Presser Company, Presser Place, Bryn Mawr, Pennsylvania 19010
"O Vos Omnes, Qui Transistis Per Viam" from *Lamentations of Jeremiah* by Alberto Ginastera, pp. 3–7
"When Jesus Wept" by William Billings, pp. 10–13
"Sing Joyfully" by Herman Berlinski, pp. 2–3
"Fog" from *Five Scenes* by David Epstein, p. 9
"To All, To Each" from *Carols of Death* by William Schuman, pp. 2–3
"Psalm 57" by Jean Berger, pp. 1–4
Theodore Presser (Elkan-Vogel Co., Inc.)
"Te Deum" by Vincent Persichetti, pp. 7–10
"Proverb" by Vincent Persichetti, pp. 3–4
Transcontinental Music Publishers, 1674 Broadway, New York, N.Y. 10019
"Psalm of Brotherhood" by Heinrich Schalit, pp. 2–5
"The 23rd Psalm" by Herbert Fromm, pp. 2–3
"Hanukkah" from *Six Madrigals* by Herbert Fromm, pp. 22–23
Walton Music Corporation, 17 West 60 Street, New York, N.Y. 10023
"Propter Magnam Gloriam" from *Gloria* by Antonio Vivaldi, pp. 32–35
"Psalm 77" by Knut Nystedt, pp. 3–5, 10–11

Composer Index

Title Index